India & Pakistan

A Mission Study
for 2005-2006

Glory Dharmaraj

Study Guide by
Diane Miller

General Board of Global Ministries • The United Methodist Church

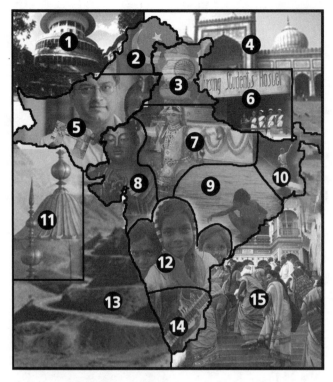

Photo Credits: Front Cover:

 1 United Christian Hospital in Lahore, Pakistan (John C. Goodwin)
 2 National Flag of Pakistan
 3 National Flag of India
 4 The Jama Masjid Mosque, New Delhi, India (John C. Goodwin)
 5 Professor Vijay Chandru with Vinay Deshpande (AP Photo/Namas Bhojani)
 6 Nursing Students Hostel at Christian Medical College Hospital, Vellore, India (Toge Fujihira)
 7 Rajustan dancer, India (Orna Golan)
 8 Statue of Buddah (Orna Golan)
 9 Puja on the Ganges, India (Orna Golan)
10 Bathing in the Ganges, India (Orna Golan)
11 Mosque in Pakistan (John C. Goodwin)
12 Varanasi children (Orna Golan)
13 Khyber Pass (John C. Goodwin)
14 Woman playing sitar, India (Orna Golan)
15 Varanasi women (Orna Golan)

Cover Design: Marcy Kass

India & Pakistan copyright ©2005 General Board of Global Ministries
A publication of the General Board of Global Ministries, The United Methodist Church

ISBN#1-890569-90-9

Library of Congress Control Number 2005920651

CONTENTS

National flag of India

National flag of Pakistan

ACKNOWLEDGMENTS

My acknowledgment is due to Rev. Dr. Toby Gould, Project Manager of Mission Studies, General Board of Global Ministries of The United Methodist Church, for his sustained interest in and moral support for my writing of this mission study. From its conceptual stage to its final draft, Toby showed a deep sensitivity and kind flexibility.

My thanks are due to Lois M. Dauway, Assistant General Secretary, the Section of Christian Social Responsibility, Women's Division, for allowing me to take time off from my office site to do research and writing for a few weeks in March and April of 2004.

I also acknowledge my colleagues, Karen Prudente, Dr. Cherian Thomas, Rebecca Asedillo, and Tamara Walker, who provided me with helpful contacts and updates for the study. I thank Carolyn Simms for her time in reading the manuscript and making helpful editorial suggestions.

I thank my husband, Raj, for his additional theological and missiological insights. I acknowledge the memory of my mother, Ranji Paul, who always believed in the education of a girl child. She put me through a university education at a time when the female literacy rate in India was 11.6 percent. Writing still is a luxury for a woman in the Global South.

My gratitude goes to the General Board of Global Ministries of The United Methodist Church for publishing this book for the mission studies of local congregations. I dedicate this Mission Study of 2005 and 2006 to the work and impact of 150 years of Methodist mission and heritage (1856-2006) in the subcontinent of India.

An Affirmation of Faith: The Common Mat of God's Grace

By Glory Dharmaraj

I believe in God the Almighty
The Ancient One who spoke through the
    silence of eternity
And uttered the earth and the heavens into
    existence.

I believe in Jesus Christ
who embraced the cycle of our existence—
even birth, growth, and death—
and offered us the Resurrection as
    the Way Out.
I believe in the Holy Spirit
who touches us with the winged noise
    of the bird—
who fills our parched existence with the
showers of the first monsoon.

I hear the Primal Sound of God
in the stillness of the snow-capped Himalayas,
the clapping waves of the Indian Ocean;

And the winds that embrace the mountains
and valleys, deserts, and rivers, between the
East and the West, the North and the South.

I hear the sound of the sandal-clad feet
    of Jesus
walking on the dusty roads to the Common
    Wells of villages
And I see him swing open the doors to all
regardless of caste, creed, and color.

I believe in the Christ
who offers us Living Waters
And leads us all on his "Yatra"* of faith
    and love
Into God's Household, Life in its Fullness.

I believe in the Great Day of Harmony
    and Balance
when all sounds and silences of our being
    and becoming
will form One Great Orchestra
in God's Great Banquet Hall.

I believe also in the Common Mat
    of God's Grace
spread across God's Household
where we will take off our shoes
in wonder and awe, and sit at God's Feast.
Until then, we commit ourselves
To be healers of the broken and crushed,
restorers of full humanity to every one,
makers of peace with the Earth,
stewards of the cosmos and our own bodies.

Therefore, we commit ourselves every day
to the Day of God's Bountiful Feast
when all God's children will be seated
around, healed and whole,
On the Common Mat of God's Grace. Amen.

* "Yatra": a journey or pilgrimage.

INTRODUCTION:
PASSAGES TO INDIA AND PAKISTAN

"Don't walk in front of me...I might not follow.

Don't walk behind me...I might not lead.

Please walk beside me and be a friend." [1]

In history and travelogue, in myth and romance, eager writers, corporate traders, and warring generals have aspired to capture the "distant" and the "different" in freeze frames of exotic landscapes and the imperial presence for readers at home. Imagination, myth, and fantasy have given rise to a multitude of images of the Indian subcontinent.

The people of India and Pakistan live in geographical locales, but the ideas and images of these real places have their own reality. Westerners view the Indian subcontinent through the lenses of a changing kaleidoscope: Anglo-Saxon literary India, the exotic India of German Romanticism, Portuguese India, Mughal India, British India, American Transcendentalists' India, post-colonial India/Pakistan, the India of the hippies, the India of information technology, and the Pakistan of the Global War Against Terrorism, to name a few. Each is an accurate snapshot, but no one emphasis can give a complete picture of the Indo/Pakistani story.

While retaining some of the features of the customary focuses of the Indo-Pakistan story—culture and customs, history and religions, including Kashmir, the religio-political bone of contention—this study limits itself to exploring India/Pakistan through the lenses of Christian mission education. This is done to foster an ongoing exchange of cultural understandings, mutuality in mission partnerships, networking with non-governmental organizations, and celebrations of border crossings against the narrow divisive walls of caste, race, gender, custom, religiosity, and social structures.

History is story, not just the analysis of events and the way they unfolded, but how those events were experienced by those whose lives were shaped by living that history. Stories overlap and amplify and correct each other. Underlying all these stories is the complexly-knit social fabric of a multicultural and multireligious subcontinent. Past and present, India is more than just a nation. It is a nation of nations, peoples of different races, and ethnicities practicing many diverse religions. To know the subcontinent is to hear the stories of the conquered as well as the conquerors, of the marginalized as well as those on the inside, of the underside as well as the sunny side.

Our study will explore the existing links of the friendships and partnerships between The United Methodist Church in the United States, the Methodist Church in India, and the United Church of Pakistan. It is a celebration of the mutuality of mission and of a coming of age. It is also an invitation to walk in solidarity with the churches in India and Pakistan, minority churches in a majority culture. It is a call to walk beside these churches and be a friend. These are the selected perspectives of passages to India and Pakistan adopted in this mission study: the strides the church has made, the odds the church faces, and the newly-forged identity the church is fashioning out of the plurality of religious neighborhoods.

A taxi passes over a bridge on the Srinagar-Muzaffarbad highway at Sheeri, India, November 2003. The highway, as well as the region and its families, has been divided since 1947 when India and Pakistan gained independence from Britain.

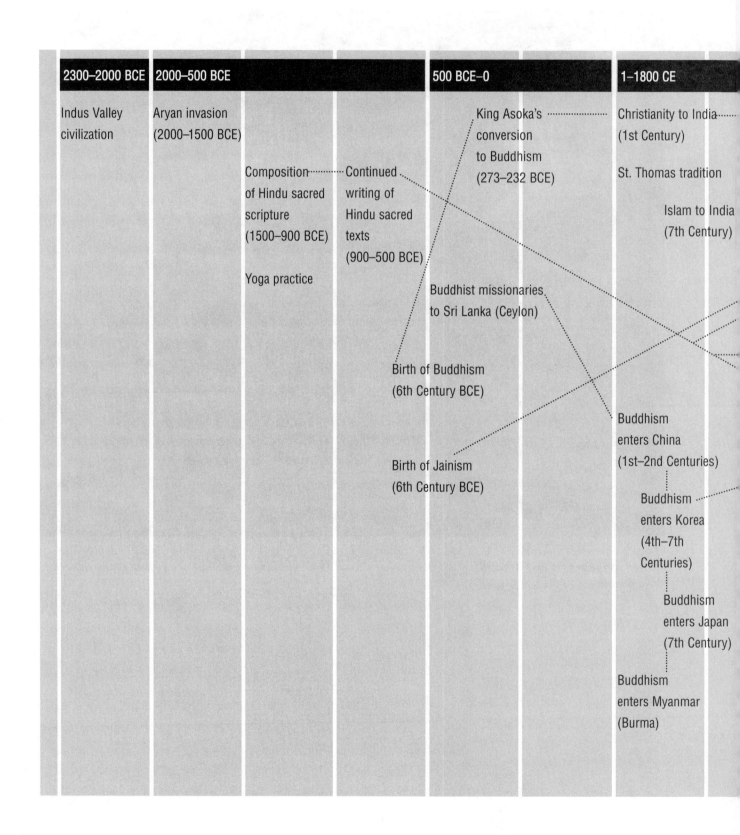

2300–2000 BCE	2000–500 BCE		500 BCE–0	1–1800 CE
Indus Valley civilization	Aryan invasion (2000–1500 BCE)		King Asoka's conversion to Buddhism (273–232 BCE)	Christianity to India (1st Century)
		Composition of Hindu sacred scripture (1500–900 BCE)	Continued writing of Hindu sacred texts (900–500 BCE)	St. Thomas tradition
				Islam to India (7th Century)
	Yoga practice		Buddhist missionaries to Sri Lanka (Ceylon)	
			Birth of Buddhism (6th Century BCE)	Buddhism enters China (1st–2nd Centuries)
			Birth of Jainism (6th Century BCE)	Buddhism enters Korea (4th–7th Centuries)
				Buddhism enters Japan (7th Century)
				Buddhism enters Myanmar (Burma)

19th Century	20th Century	21st Century

Western Protestant mission to India

Influence of Hinduism

Influence of Christianity

Influence of Jainism

Translations of Buddhists' sacred texts in Europe
(Late 19th Century)

American Transcendentalists
Ralph Waldo Emerson,
Henry David Thoreau,
Walt Whitman
(19th Century)

World Parliament of Religions in Chicago
(1893: Swami Vivekanadanda's speech on Hinduism and its impact on the United States)

Mahatma Gandhi

(Peace and non-violence)

The Rev. Dr. Martin Luther King, Jr.
The Rev. David Lawrence

E. Stanley Jones

(Ashram Movement)

Zen Buddhist school of thought in the United States

Yoga practices
Meditation

Hippies
(Selected strands of Hinduism)

Eco-spirituality
Saving the earth
(Influence of major religions)

Centenary of World Parliament of Religions (1993)

Proposal of a global ethic

Civil disobedience

Peace movement

Christian Ashram in the United States

Yoga practices
Meditation

New Age movement
(Selected strands from classical Hinduism)

2004 World Parliament of Religions in Spain

Peace with earth

The Hindu goddess Kali fighting Oeman depicted in relief, Majabali, India. Kali is the destructive and creative aspect of God as the Divine Mother in Hinduism.

1

ANCIENT ROOTS OF THE SUBCONTINENT

PASSAGE TO INDIA!

...LO SOUL, THE RETROSPECT
BROUGHT FORWARD;

THE OLD, MOST POPULOUS,
WEALTHIEST OF
EARTH'S LANDS,

THE STREAMS OF THE INDUS
AND THE GANGES, AND THEIR
MANY AFFLUENTS;

(I, MY SHORES OF AMERICA
WALKING TODAY, BEHOLD,
RESUMING ALL)

—WALT WHITMAN,
EXCERPT FROM *"PASSAGE TO INDIA"*

Walt Whitman wrote these lines in his poem, "Passage to India," a delightful expedition of a soul toward its homeland, God. He wrote the poem soon after three major engineering and technological feats that brought peoples of the globe together in the nineteenth century: the laying of a telephone cable across the Atlantic Ocean, the building of the transcontinental railroad across the United States, and the opening of the Suez Canal in the Middle East. In his own sweeping inimitable style, Whitman calls the year 1869, "the year of the marriage of continents, climates and oceans." The underside of this history, however, is the story of the imported Chinese laborers who struggled to complete the transcontinental railroad across America in 1869. Technological and engineering accomplishments often required the exploitation of a cheap labor force.

On the national scene, other epoch-making events were taking place. That was the year when two secular women's organizations were formed to work for women's right to vote. The National Woman Suffrage Association, led by Elizabeth Cady Stanton and Susan B. Anthony, and the American Women

Suffrage Association, led by Lucy Stone and Julia Ward Howe, opened new doors for women. It was also the year of the birth of the United Methodist Women's predecessor organization, Methodist Woman's Foreign Missionary Society. In that year the first single female missionaries to India, Isabella Thoburn, an educator, and Dr. Clara Swain, a medical doctor, were sent there to work among India's women and children.

This chapter explores the ancient roots of the culture and peoples of the subcontinent. From these ancient roots sprang up a faith and a body of religious writings that would profoundly impact not only the saga of the Indian subcontinent, but a considerable body of Western religious thought into the nineteenth and twentieth centuries. These deep roots are also the source of

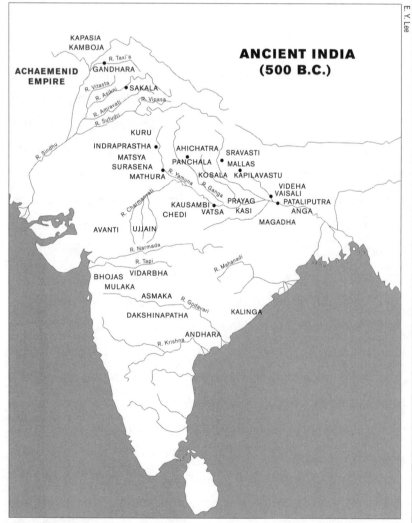

Map of Ancient India in 500 BCE

India and Pakistan: "midnight children," born less than a day apart, destined to seek forever to settle the destructive battles of an unresolved sibling rivalry.

Civilizations flourish by rivers and in coastal valleys. In fact, this is true of civilization in America even today. According to the 2000 census, the majority of Americans, about 53 percent or some 148 million people, live in coastal areas. It is projected that these areas will grow by nearly 50 percent during the next twelve years.[1]

*Indian legend has it that before the Indian River Ganges came into existence and when the earth was still arid, there was a wise king. This ancient king, Bhagirath (**BAA gi raath**), meditated day and night on a stone in order to bring down the Ganges from its abode in the Himalayas. His prayers were heard and the waters of the Ganges broke loose from the heights of the Himalayas in a mighty torrential rush.*

In order to slow down the great torrents of water beating down on the heretofore arid and naked earth, the Hindu god, Shiva, helped break the force of the waters with the locks of his hair. This story, descending in slow trickles from Aryan India to modern India, is still celebrated by the worshipers of Mother Ganges in April and during the fall each year.

entrenched attitudes and patterns of behavior toward those on the margins of society.

This chapter examines the sunny side as well as the underside of history. It is the story of India and of Pakistan as well, until 1947, the year of partition and the year of independence for both countries. The two countries are "midnight children," born less than a day apart, destined to seek forever to settle the destructive battles of an unresolved sibling rivalry.

EXCAVATING THE ROOTS OF HISTORY

Roughly around the time when the transcontinental railroad was being constructed across the United States, British engineers and Indian construction workers were building railroads in India. In one such enterprise in the northwest of India, workers encountered huge mounds that hid burnt bricks. The bricks being used to build the railroad yielded a long-hidden archeological secret. What was concealed beneath the bricks was a conspiracy of sand and water, flood tides and landslides, which had stealthily hidden the labor of a vast and long extinct civilization, the Indus Valley Civilization. The name India is derived from the river Indus. The Indus Valley Civilization covered most of what is now Pakistan.

Beneath the bricks unearthed by the Indian construction workers in the mid-nineteenth century lay the remains of a culture even older than that of Abraham. Neatly designed Indian streets in grid patterns, heavy brick walls, a written script, granaries, pottery created on pottery wheels, and evidence of the use of cotton and yarn revealed a sophisticated urban civilization.

The story of ancient India has its origin far back across the span of history at around 2500 BCE (Before the Common Era), when the "first nation," the original inhabitants of the land, were living there. In 1932 an archaeological dig at Ur, the original home of our biblical ancestors Abraham, Sarah, and Hagar, revealed that Ur of Sumeria, in the Euphrates and Tigris River valleys in modern-day Iraq, had a trade relationship with the Indus River valley in India. This was even before the period of

Abraham, Sarah, and Hagar, who lived out their lives of faith and struggle around 2000 BCE.

God called Abraham from Ur of Sumer, which, like the Indus Valley culture, also had a written script, the use of wheels, neatly-arranged gridded cities, and trade relationships, in order to go on a faith journey. It was a pilgrim's quest, probably undertaken on donkeys and mules. There were other journeys taken by other peoples—not faith journeys, but journeys of conquest. Journeys of faith and journeys of conquest criss-cross throughout history, forming overlapping histories of warfare and the sacred.

The Aryan Invasion

The original inhabitants of the Indus River valley, whose descendants still live in modern-day Pakistan and northwest India, were invaded by Aryans who came on horseback, an advanced military transport at that time. These conquerors came through the imposing yet vulnerable Himalayan passes. The Indus valley inhabitants only had domesticated camels, goats, water buffaloes, and elephants.

Since that time innumerable fierce battles have taken place in this river valley over the fertile arable land and richly silted terrain. The invading forces overran and destroyed the highly developed civic structures and agricultural societies, the trade connections with the outside world, and the exchange of coin systems of the pre-Aryan culture. The invaders gradually took over the sophisticated culture of India, subordinating its original inhabitants and dominating the subcontinent's culture, ethos, and religions. The pre-Aryan people's darker skins were different from the light-skinned Aryan invaders. Later the pre-Aryans would be called slaves or "dasas."

A comparable time frame from biblical history will help situate this piece of Indian history (roughly from 2000-600 BCE) for readers of this mission study. The Indian period of Aryan invasion and the following years when the Aryans created their major religious and epic writings begins at the time of

In contrast to New Age thought, Christian belief deals with sin and redemption, as well as the healing and restoration of both individual and corporate selves. What New Age thinking has exposed is a deep-felt need in our culture to experience God. In United Methodist Women's terms, we must know God and experience freedom as whole persons in Jesus Christ. In church language, it is the need for theology to be undergirded with spirituality and reinforced by "neighborology," to use the phrase of theologian Kosuke Koyama.

Abraham, Sarah, and Hagar (2000 BCE). It extends through the time of the Exodus when Moses led the slaves to freedom (1260 BCE), and forward to the era of Saul, David, and Solomon, to just before Jerusalem fell to Babylon (587/586 BCE).

The writer of Chronicles even records the trade relationship King Solomon had with the region of India and Sri Lanka during this period. Gold, silver, ivory, apes, and peacocks were some of the trade commodities recorded both in the Bible (II Chronicles 9:21) and in Tamil literature, the most ancient language and literature of South India.

THE IMPACT OF ANCIENT HINDU SCRIPTURES AND WRITINGS

A prayer which has come down from this ancient period is an example of the spirituality recorded in the Hindu mystical writings called *Upanishads* (1500–500 BCE):

> Lead us from the unreal to the real
>
> From darkness to light
>
> From death to immortality
>
> *(Brihadaranyaka Upanishad)*

The Aryans produced an extensive body of religious and philosophical texts in Sanskrit. These writings, called Vedas (**VE daas**), have subsumed almost every other aspect of Indian history and dominate the consciousness of historians at the expense of the land's other histories. The period between 1000 BCE and 600 BCE is known as the Vedic Age, reflecting the predominance of the Vedas.

One of the major Hindu concepts of God which emerged during this period is that of the Absolute, the Ultimate Reality, or the World Soul, otherwise known as Brahman (**BRAAH man**).[2] Brahman should not be confused with Brahmin, one of the castes in Indian social hierarchy.

The World Soul is in all things present—in all aspects of nature, and also present in the human soul. The divine essence of the human soul is identical with the World Soul. In Brahman,

The religious and philosophical links of thought and practice between Vedic India and nineteenth- and twentieth-century thought in our society are an intriguing phenomenon. It is worth noting that much of the original American Transcendentalist activity was centered in the Boston area, where the seeds of United Methodist Women's history were also being sown in the nineteenth century. It is a curious coincidence of East-West parallel influences, with opposite target audiences.

all contradictions merge: emptiness and fullness, positives and negatives exist as two sides of the same coin. All dualities are non-existent. In this concept of God, the World Soul is not responsible for good and evil.

According to the Hindu concept of salvation, Moksha (**Mok SHAA**) or liberation, comes through the merger of the human soul, Atman (**Aat MAAN**) with the World Soul, Brahman. Before such a union takes place, the human soul has to go through reincarnation, an endless cycle of existence and rebirths.

The Law of Karma (**kar MAA**), the weighing scale of good and evil, determines how many lives one is bound to live and what forms of life one has to take on. To be born human is to rise high in the cycle of births. To be born a Brahmin is a still greater spiritual achievement. Karma, one's deeds in this life, determines one's future birth.

Both life and history are conceptualized in terms of cycles in this view of life and salvation. The wheel is a major religious and philosophical symbol. It represents existence with its continuous change and contains an immovable still point at the center as the focal point. Since liberation is to escape the endless wheel of existence, the concept of persons as change agents in history is missing in this notion of cyclical history.

The religious and philosophical thought of this Indian Vedic Period is reflected in the writings of American Transcendentalists, which burst upon the intellectual landscape of nineteenth-century America. Transcendentalism, a movement based on Eastern thought, gave priority to individual spiritual insight and instincts over reason and dogma, and to belief in the innate goodness of human beings over concepts of original sin.

Ralph Waldo Emerson (1803-1882), Henry David Thoreau (1817-1862) and Walt Whitman (1819-1892) found their inspiration and thought in the classical Hinduism of the Vedic Period. Later on in the 1960s, hippies and others, such as the Beatles and their followers, were drawn to the impact of Hindu transcendentalism.

Comparable to the Greek epic works, The Iliad *and* The Odyssey, *are two of the epics of ancient India,* Mahabharata *(Ma HAA bhaa rata) and* Ramayana *(Ra MAA yana), composed during the period between 600 and 500 BCE.* Mahabharata *is an epic story of chivalry and fighting, of the imperial code of conduct and the royal surrender to common temptation. It is a story of how the hero, Dharmaraja (King of the Code of Conduct), in a frenzy of gambling, loses not only his kingdom and the inheritance of his noble brothers, but also his lovely wife, Draupadi (drau pat EE), who was married to all the five brothers as well.*

A part of this vast national epic is the Hindu scripture Bhagavad Gita, the Song of the Adorable One. Bhagavad Gita is a story of a war between bad guys and good guys, in which a Hindu god directs a distraught warrior-prince in the war. Even today, mainstream Hindus read it as a spiritual struggle between the good and evil in one's soul, while those who interpret the text more narrowly view it as endorsing war and ethnic cleansing in the land.

The Ramayana *is a story about an ideal Indian king, Rama, and his wife, Sita. Due to court intrigues, Rama was exiled before his coronation as king, and his brother became the king. Rama and Sita spent years in a forest. Sita, abducted by the giant king of Sri Lanka, was imprisoned in a beautiful grove guarded by the king's harem. She was neither injured nor violated by her royal abductor.*

Finally, after overcoming many obstacles, Rama assumed royal leadership and ruled in a place called Ayodhya in India. However, Sita had to prove her sexual purity to her subjects and to her husband by literally walking through coals of fire. She passed the ordeal by fire and thus became the symbol of the ideal wife.

In a different way, followers of the current New Age movement are now being impacted. Consciously or not, the movement derives many of the strands of its thinking from the classical period of Hinduism. The New Age movement also posits that everything is God, and God is the "Ultimate Unifying Principle." Distinctions like God, creation, and humanity are illusions, since all are one. God is more an energy, force, and light than a personality.

When one is enlightened about one's real identity, then God-realization or self-realization or illumination of consciousness, that is, Nirvana, takes place. The New Age movement focuses on experience that transforms consciousness: a therapeutic religion to its seekers.

The image of Sita is a powerful force in Indian politics as well as in the psyche of Indian women. So is the place called Ayodhya where Rama ruled, a site sacred for the Hindus, since Rama is venerated as a god. This is where Babri Masjid, a Muslim mosque, was demolished on December 6, 1992. Religious sectarian riots have continued to disrupt the social fabric since then. Muslim and Hindu relations have yet to be restored.

ANCIENT HISTORY, WRITINGS, AND CASTE

A knowledge of ancient India today is necessary in order to understand the current social, and in some cases, political impact of this period in India in the context of religion, race, and gender. While wisdom and inspiration are imparted by the various religious texts of that period, there are also deeply-entrenched attitudes that have contributed to the subordination of certain groups of people. This is the underside of the history of the subcontinent.

The role of social divisions known as castes has been impacted by the writings and arrangement of society reflected in the Vedic Period. Acutely conscious of racial superiority, the Aryans divided society into four major castes based on colors or Varnas (**Var NAAS**). That done, a whole set of notions of human purity and pollution came into social existence.

According to a hymn called "Purusasukta" in the *Rig Veda*, four castes were created from God's own body: the Brahmin (priestly class) was created from God's mouth, the Kshatriya (warriors and rulers) from his arms, the Vaishyas (traders and crafts people) from his thighs, and the Shudra (those who serve the other three castes) from his feet.

There were other people who were completely outside these four castes. They were the so-called "untouchables," today's Dalits, a people broken to the core by this system of social arrangement. The word "dalit" comes from the Sanskrit word "dal" which means "broken," a name willingly assumed by the six million Dalits in India to protest their historically down-trodden condition. These untouchables, who were not part of the four-fold division and therefore not even considered part of the body of God, were assigned to tasks considered menial in the Indian subcontinent—cleaning and removing dirt and human waste, tanning animal skins, and so on.

Though changes have been brought about by social and political movements, constitutional guarantees, and the process of urbanization, the impact left by casteism, an act of racism endorsed by the theory of chosen race, is deeply felt. History's underside is extremely painful but it is something to be confronted and addressed (see Chapter 4 for a discussion of the Dalit question and Chapter 5 for Dalit theology, including interviews with two female Dalit theologians in India).

ANCIENT HISTORY, WRITINGS, AND THE ROLE AND STATUS OF WOMEN

Ancient religious texts have had a pervasive impact on the role and status of women as well. Women are put on pedestals as goddesses, but treated as less than equals when it comes to the gender division of labor in private and public spheres.

From ancient days, India's rivers have been called by female names. Two of the best known are the Ganges in the north and Kauveri (**KAA veri**) in the south. Sacred hymns written by gifted

---

Reincarnation:
an endless cycle of existence and rebirths

Karma:
one's deeds in this life and their consequences

Nirvana:
God-realization, self-realization, or illumination of consciousness

CASTES CONSTRUCTED AS GOD'S BODY PARTS:

Brahmin
(priestly class):
God's mouth

Kshatriya
(warriors and rulers):
God's arms

Vaishyas
(traders and crafts people):
God's thighs

Shudra
(those who serve the other three castes):
God's feet

—The *Rig Veda*

women were included in the earliest of writings, the *Rig Veda*. But the ancient tradition of the dependence of a woman on her father while she was in her parents' house, dependence on her husband when married, and then dependence on her son when a widow, has been passed down by patriarchy and internalized by women. Chapter 4 will explore these issues further, along with the various forms of marriages endorsed by ancient texts, and the prevalence of dowry even today in both India and Pakistan as a powerful vestige of one of the marriage forms.

ANCIENT HISTORY, WRITINGS, AND POLITICS

Unlike the other geographical mission studies, ancient history is important here because the history of Aryan invasion and the writings which sprang up in its wake continue to be manipulated not only for race and gender purposes, but also for political motives. An extremist Hindu movement called Hindutva (**Hin DUT vaa**), with its resurgence in the 1980s, has been exploiting the Indian landscape through its Hindu nationalism and a narrow interpretation of Hinduism.

Hindutva should not be confused with Hinduism. Hindutva claims an identity called Hindu-ness, while Hinduism is a religion. Hindutva is to Hinduism what an ideological and politically motivated sect or cult is to a religion. To draw a rough analogy, what the Christian Identity Movement is to Christianity in the United States, Hindutva is to Hinduism.

Hindutva can be described as Hindu religious sectarianism or Hindu nationalism. Hindutva provided the basic motivation for the demolition of the Muslim mosque in Ayodhya. The cult of Hindutva is professed by powerful political groups and the former ruling party in India, the Hindu-nationalist Bharatiya Janata Party (BJP).

According to this Hindu nationalistic argument, Aryans did not migrate from outside India, but they were the "indigenous children of the soil always." The Hindu and the Aryan are the same. "Hindutva is described as 'Cultural Nationalism,' to which Indian people are required to subscribe preferably under

In both India and Pakistan, the highest administrative offices have been held by two famous women, Indira Gandhi and Benazir Butto, respectively. In the Indian elections of 2004, the Congress Party led by Sonia Gandhi was elected. Though many in her party expected her to become the Prime Minister, she steered the political and good will of the Indian National Congress toward the choice of another person. Manmohan Singh, an economist, became the Prime Minister of India in the spring of 2004 to lead a coalition government. But gender equality is still a struggle interlaced with contradictions.

Hindu dictatorship." [3] In this argument, Christians and Muslims are portrayed as the "other."

The land is redefined as a holy land for its own religion, which is an affront to the secularism promised in India's constitution to all the inhabitants of the land, including Christians and Muslims. Exploited by extremists, Hindutva has been an ideological and political weapon against minority religious groups.

ROMANTICIZING ANCIENT HISTORY AND WRITINGS

It is tempting to romanticize history. The same period of history following the Aryan invasion of India was romanticized by some eighteenth-century Germans. August Schlegel (1767-1845), a German poet, along with several leading writers of the period, saw in this ancient India a utopia that could help revitalize Europe. He said, "It is in the Orient that we (Europe) should search for its highest Romanticism." [4] The German Romantics elevated this period as an antidote to European materialism and acquisitiveness.

The longing for a purist past, the "good old days" of some other culture or of one's own culture, is at best wishful thinking and at worst a potential seedbed for exclusionary acts. There is no such thing as a purist past. At the same time, such a constructed world can be manipulated in order to exclude a group of people. That is what also happened in Germany.

Pan-Germanism as an ideology used the notion that the Sanskrit language was older than Hebrew to incite anti-Semitism in Europe. To romanticize one culture can sometimes lead to demonizing another, for the tendencies to romanticize and to demonize can be closely related. Histories and languages can be exploited to make a people an "other" and an enemy.

CULTURE, RELIGION, AND LANGUAGE STUDIES: FOR GOOD OR ILL

Often religions have ambiguities. So it falls on the faithful, whether they be Christian or adherents of other world religions, to seek life-giving, life-affirming principles from a religion and to

Secular thinkers and spiritual leaders have always sought to reread and redress history to improve humanity. They have identified positive elements and reread religious texts in favor of peace and non-violence. A famous example of such a person is Mahatma Gandhi. Gandhi intentionally used the religion and history of this period for positive and harmonious living and liberation from oppression. Though the base of his spirituality came principally from Hindu scriptures, he incorporated other scriptural truths for the cause of peace and non-violence.

In his copy of the Hindu scripture, the Baghavat Gita *(a warrior text embedded in* Mahabharata)*, he wrote that "perfect renunciation" was impossible without "perfect observance of ahimsa (non-violence) in every shape and form." [5]*

use these principles for the good of all God's peoples and creation itself. In part, that is what it means to engage in an interfaith endeavor. It is a bridge-building effort, needed now more than ever.

An enterprise seeking commonality among languages was taken up by language experts in the nineteenth century. These philologists, including William Jones, Jacob Grimms, famed writer of children's stories, and Franz Bopp, examined the common roots of languages like Sanskrit, Latin, and Greek. Even today, comparative linguistics in both the West and East points to the ancestral roots of all these languages. Old English, the language of *Beowulf*, has a common linguistic ancestry with Sanskrit of ancient India. While such studies can be a way to build bridges, the same study has been interpreted narrowly by others in the past for negative purposes.

Resistance to using language, culture, medical studies, and religion to subordinate one group of people to another must be part of one's advocacy efforts. It is an act of eternal vigilance. Thereby, one becomes part of a group of people which consciously sets out to preserve the positives in the study of languages, cultures, anthropology, sciences, and religions, while opposing and abandoning death-dealing forces. Caution must be exercised against any uncritical acceptance of what goes on in the name of study of culture, religion, and language.

Taj Mahal, mausoleum of Mughal empress Mumtaz Mahal, in Agra, India.

East-West Philosophy in a Nutshell

Eastern philosophical thought may seem diametrically opposed to Western thinking in how it grasps reality. East and West are often reduced to two simplistic categories of thought behavior: "being" and "becoming." The following reading is a dialog between the two. It offers the opportunity to taste the flavors of ancient philosophical thoughts.

A Reading on Being and Becoming: From a Dualistic Vision to a Holistic Vision

READER 1

I am on a journey.

My name is BECOMING.

How DO you do?

I am DOING fine.

Doing is the main goal in my journey.

Moving from point A to point B by the shortest route is my focus.

My journey has an origin and a destination. It is a linear journey.

My thought is linear.
I think on a straight line of progressive stages.

I am motion.

A shaft of energy.

Two modalities.

Two ways of living.

I am empirical. I am a problem solver.

I am mono-dimensional.

You know what your problem is?
You are cluttered and convoluted.

READER 2

I am on a journey.

My name is BEING.

How ARE you?

I AM fine.

Being is the main goal in my journey.

The journey itself is my focus.

My journey is relational and cyclical. "The journey is home."[7]

I think in patterns.
I think on a spiral of continuous developing potentialities.[8]

I am stillness.

A field of awareness.

Two ways of knowing.

Two ways of loving.

I apprehend reality through imagination and perception.

I am multi-dimensional.

You know what your problem is?
You reduce everything to cause and effect.
You are trapped in time.

You are afraid of time—that is what it is. You put effect first and cause afterwards.

I am sequential.

How circular!

I am an individual, and I take control of myself.

How awfully slow that must be!

I am for rational understanding and learning.

You are likely to end up as a teary-eyed bleeding heart.

But listen. I have a God. My God said, "I am the Alpha and Omega" (Revelation 22:13). My God is the God of forward strokes.

My God affirms "becoming."

I am for ministry as the transforming agency in the world.

Do we happen to worship the same God?

The God of *becoming*.

The One who *became* a child.

You know what? I begin to *think* the same God who is in me may be in you, too.

You mean the One who *became* one among us?

One Lord.

With a "Go-Between God" in Christ.[9]

On the other hand, I am not reduced by the tyranny of time.

I am simultaneous.

How linear!

I am a connected self, part of a collective entity. The communal self takes control of me.

How dangerously fast that must be!

I am for affective and connected knowing and learning.

You are likely to end up in your water-tight rational aloofness.

I have a God. My God said, "I AM who I AM" (Exodus 3:14). Jesus said, "Before Abraham was born, I AM (John 8:58)." My God is the God of forward and backward and sideways as well.

My God affirms "being."

I am for living the incarnational ministry of the *Word*.

Do we?

The God of Being.

The One who was, who is, and ever shall be.

You know what? I begin to *feel* the same God who is in me may be in you, too.

You mean the One who is the "Ground of our *being*"?

One Spirit.

In the in-betweenness of our lives.

READER 1	READER 2
Then let us name the history that blindfolded us.	Let us name that history that blindsided us.
Into historic splits.	Into historic wounds.
Pitting body against soul.	Setting mind against matter.
For the sake of fullness of Life (John 10:10).	For the sake of wholeness of perspective.
Let us correct our visions.	Heal our spirits.
And celebrate our constant becomings in life and death.	And celebrate our gifts of being and presence.
In life and death. For in our entry and exit, you and I are the same.	In life and death. In our entry and exit, you and I are the same.
So let us celebrate one another. And let us celebrate the God of Complementarity.[10]	Let us celebrate one another. And celebrate the God of Complementarity.
In Christ, there is no East or West.	In Christ, there is no West or East.
My name is Becoming.	My name is Being.

Differing world views can co-exist together if we look for possible commonalities. In order to exercise a balanced approach to studying history, whether our own or the history of someone else, we need to be aware of likely pitfalls and avoid them.

The Khyber Pass, shown here, is a thirty-three mile passage through the Hindu Kush mountain range, which connects the northern frontier of Pakistan with Afghanistan. "Khyber" means "across the river" or "divide," and is derived from "Haber" in Aramaic, which also translates to the word "Hebrew."

2

FROM TRADE ROUTES TO TRADE COMPANIES

I ASK MYSELF NOW

WHY I DO NOT LIMIT MY LOVE

TO THE SUDDEN ROSES,

THE TIDES OF JUNE,

THE MOONS OVER THE SEA?

WHY HAVE I HAD TO LOVE THE

ROSE *AND* JUSTICE,

THE SEA *AND* JUSTICE,

JUSTICE *AND* THE LIGHT?

—JUAN GONZALO ROSE
IN "CARTA A MARIA TERESA"[1]

This chapter seeks to articulate a vast span of history on the Indian subcontinent through the stories of the birth of three major religions, Buddhism, Jainism, and Sikhism, and the arrival of two others, Christianity and Islam. The aim is also to give a kaleidoscopic view of the history of colonization, glimpsing it through stories of selected major figures, major trade routes, and major events.

Imagine a vast time period, with the help of landmarks in biblical history as well as European history. The first leg of this journey, from 600 BCE to the first Christmas, will be compressed in the next few pages. Our walk will take us from the Babylonian captivity of Israel and deportations to Babylon in 597 to 582 BCE, and from the dedication of the second temple at Jerusalem in 515 BCE to Herod's rebuilding of this temple in 19 BCE, to the birth of Jesus Christ.

This time period also saw the empire of Greeks, the writings of Socrates, Plato, and Aristotle (427-322 BCE), and the conquests of Alexander the Great (336-323 BCE) when he spread Greek culture from Asia Minor to India. This period saw the rise of the Roman Empire (100-63 BCE) and the intrigues of romance and politics of Julius Caesar and Mark Antony with Cleopatra (51-30 BCE). It was the era that saw the spread of the Roman Empire. In this time period Augustus Caesar issued his decree mandating a census just before the birth of Jesus, and Jesus was born in Bethlehem in Palestine, a Roman colony.

THE BIRTH OF THREE FAITHS

Two major religious figures protested against the social and religious evils of India. They were the founders of Buddhism and Jainism, Gautama the Buddha (563 BCE), and Mahavira (**Ma haa VEE raa**) the Brave (540-468 BCE). Both leaders protested against the misrule and dominance by Brahmins in religion and society. They advocated for social equality, justice, peace, and freedom. Rejecting the Vedas, rituals, and sacrifices, they worked for non-violence and love. Coming from royal and warrior families, respectively, the Buddha and Mahavira espoused these central truths after they encountered societal injustices and experienced such inevitable losses as the death of loved ones and the pain of sickness and decay.

Buddhism

In the sixth century BCE, Buddhism started as a movement of reform against the caste system and the domination of Brahmins in the practices of Hinduism. The essence of Buddhism lies in the Four Noble Truths and an Eightfold Path to Enlightenment. The Four Noble Truths speak to life being rooted in suffering, the cause of suffering (desire), the cessation of suffering, and the path leading to the end of suffering.

For Gautama the Buddha, founder of Buddhism, there were two extremes to be avoided on the road to salvation. On the one hand, one must avoid a life given to the pursuit of fleeting desires, passions, and pleasures. But one should also avoid a life given to self-mortification, which is painful and fruitless. Steering through the extremes of attachment and detachment in

Threefold Commitment

I take refuge in the Buddha (the founder).

I take refuge in the Dharma (his teachings).

I take refuge in the Sangha (the organization of monks and nuns).

Fivefold Moral Principles

To abstain from killing, stealing, adultery, lying, and intoxicants.

Noble Eightfold Path

Right Understanding

Right Thoughts

Right Speech

Right Action

Right Livelihood

Right Effort

Right Mindfulness

Right Concentration

Dwight S. Busacca

Statue of Buddha untying the knot of suffering.

existence, the Middle Path, or the Noble Eightfold Path, is the secret to Enlightenment.

Therefore, Right Understanding, Right Thoughts, Right Speech (truth telling), Right Action (peaceful, pure, and honest), Right Livelihood, Right Effort (self-control), Right Mindfulness, and Right Concentration (into the deep mysteries of life) constitute the Eightfold Path to Enlightenment. Salvation (Nirvana) is to escape from the flux and wheel of existence characterized by suffering.

Buddhism is sustained by its threefold commitment: "I take refuge in the Buddha (the founder), I take refuge in the Dharma (his teachings), I take refuge in the Sangha (the organization of monks and nuns)." The fivefold moral principles of Buddhism are to abstain from killing, stealing, adultery, lying, and intoxicants. Devout followers of Buddhism recite both the threefold commitment and the fivefold moral principles twice daily in the original Pali language.

From the third century BCE, Buddhist missionaries spread their faith to countries such as Sri Lanka, China, Korea, and Japan. The twentieth century saw the increase of its adherents in the West. Though India is its homeland, Buddhism had almost died out there until the 1950s. Then the Dalits (untouchables) embraced Buddhism, as well as refugees who came from Tibet to India. The twentieth century saw the influx of Buddhism in the West.

Jainism

Jainism originated as a protest to Hinduism. Today, there are about four million followers of Jainism in India. Jainism teaches that Right Faith, Right Knowledge, and Right Conduct will lead to salvation. Right Conduct includes non-violence (ahimsa), truth telling, abstention from theft, abstention from greed, and the practice of sexual purity.

Jainism does not believe in the existence of God. A liberated soul, a prophet, is a god. Every soul is potentially divine. When the soul follows the right disciplines and the purification process, it attains salvation: liberation from Karma, one's own acts, and their consequences. A person is punished or rewarded by his own acts in a cycle of births. Such is their regard for life that some Jain ascetics carry a broom and sweep their path lest they step on any living thing and kill it.

Sikhism

Much later, Sikhism also had its birth in India. Founded in the fifteenth century by Guru Nanak, Sikhism believes in one God and rejects idol worship and caste. Guru Nanak started free community kitchens where his followers could eat together, regardless of their caste affiliations.

The Code of Conduct is stricter for Jain ascetics. The five vows:

1 Abstention from untruth

2 Abstention from violence

3 Abstention from stealing

4 Abstention from sexual engagement

5 Abstention from greed

Right Faith, Right Knowledge, and Right Conduct lead to salvation.

There is only one God.

His name is Truth.

He is the Creator.

He makes his will known to people when they meditate on the True Name and the Sacred Writings.

The way of liberation is to align one's will with the will of God.

This is possible through God's grace, "Kirpa."

Those who follow the path of God pass through certain stages: Appropriate Living, Deeper Enlightenment, Joyful Efforts, Bliss of Merging with the Divine.

These can be obtained by being a householder and not renouncing the world.

Five Evil Passions

Lust

Anger

Greed

Attachment to Earthly Possessions

Pride

In the Sikh concept of God, the sovereign God makes his will known to human beings, even though he does not appear in person. Though Karma, the law of the consequence of human actions, is at work, one can align oneself with God's will and with God's help can attain salvation. Worshiping the True Name or God is the quest of the religion. The Golden Temple in Amritsar is the holiest shrine of Sikhism.

In the seventeenth century, Sikhs endured persecution at the hands of the Moghal government in northern India. Guru Gobind Singh, leader of the Sikhs, created a group of intensely loyal Sikhs called the Khalsa, a body of initiated soldier-saints willing to die for the community if necessary. Following a strict code of moral conduct, they vowed to protect the needy by being brave in battles.

A political quest of Sikhs is the creation of a homeland for themselves. This land, Khalistan, the land of the pure, would be a place where the initiated Sikhs could become the rulers. Present-day Punjab, where the Sikhs are the majority, is the core of this envisioned land. The autonomy of such a homeland or province for Sikhs is contested since it is seen as separatism.

At the same time, there are Sikh moderates who believe in a unified India. Manmohan Singh, elected in May 2004 as the thirteenth Prime Minister of India, is the country's first Sikh prime minister and endorses an undivided India. Today there are about eighteen million Sikhs in India.

TRADE ROUTES AND THE ARRIVAL OF TWO FAITHS

India's strategic location and rich resources inevitably attracted traders who later became empire seekers and builders. Land trade routes with Antioch in Syria existed along Iraq's Tigris and Euphrates valleys, through northern Persia and Kandahar, Afghanistan, and the Khyber Pass in the Himalayas, a region that has attracted recent media attention. In the East, trade routes connected India with Indonesia and China. Spices and silk flowed along these routes.

Sea routes from Rome to India were charted through the study of trade winds and monsoons. From the first century, trade was carried on with the Roman Empire using these sea routes. Muslin, pearls, jewels, spices, and precious stones were exported as commodities. From the West and the Middle East, India imported damask, copper, lead, and tin.

The Arrival of Christianity

These land and sea routes were also pathways for the arrival of the Christian faith. Christianity was brought to India by Thomas, a disciple of Jesus. He went as a missionary to India about 52 CE (Common Era), spreading the gospel and establishing a church. He was killed in Mylapore, Chennai (Madras) for witnessing to his faith. "Thomas Church" is still part of the Christian tradition of India. The followers of this church did not spread Christianity to other parts of the land, but kept it to themselves as their own caste-bound religion. This ancient Christian church in India, the Mar Thoma Church, also has its followers in the United States. In fact, today the Mar Thoma Church is one of the member communions of the National Council of Churches in the U.S.A.

In 435 CE the Nestorians organized themselves as a church in Syria and assumed the title of Chaldean Christians (a name by which they are known even today in Iraq). Known as the Syrian Church or Chaldean Church in Persia, the Nestorians spread far and wide, as far as China in the seventh century. A large group of Christians came to India from Persia, Syria, and Mesopotamia (modern day Iraq) in 345 CE seeking refuge from the persecution of a Persian emperor against Christians.

The Arrival of Islam

Arab merchants professing Islam traded with India and then settled in several parts of the country. Founded by Mohammed (570-632 CE), Islam gave the status of "people of the Book" to both Jews and Christians.

Five Pillars of Islam

Iman or Faith
Every Muslim must testify, "There is no god but Allah, and Mohammed is his messenger."

Salah or Prayer
Every Muslim must face Mecca and pray five times a day.

Zakah or Almsgiving
Muslims are instructed to give 2.5 percent of their income and wealth to the needy.

Sawn or Fasting
Muslims are commanded to fast in the ninth lunar month of Ramadan.

Hajj or Pilgrimage
Muslims who are able are commanded to make one pilgrimage to Mecca in their lifetime.

Mughal Invasion

A wave of Turkish invasions took place in India in the eleventh and twelfth centuries. There was further territorial expansion by the invasion of Mughals. Founded by Babur in 1526 CE, over the span of a couple of centuries the Mughal Empire stretched from Kabul in the west in today's Afghanistan to Dacca in the east in today's Bangla Desh; from Kashmir in the north in today's India/Pakistan to Chennai (Madras), India in the south.

One famous Mughal emperor, Akbar (1556-1605 CE), began building Mughal architectural wonders, establishing a legacy for his successors. The Western world became interested in establishing trade in commodities such as pepper, other spices, and textiles. Akbar's immediate successor, Jahangir (1605-27 CE), received an ambassador from King James I of England.

Shah Jahan, another Mughal king (1628-58 CE), is known for some of the most famous architectural monuments including the Taj Mahal. Built by Shah Jahan in memory of his wife, Mumtaz Mahal, who bore him fourteen children and died in childbirth, this mausoleum is known as a "tender elegy in marble." Erected by the labor of slaves over a twenty-year time span for an empress who died, the Taj Mahal stands as a memorial to the labor of love and sweat. In the moonlight, the Taj is absolutely breathtaking, though not under the scorching light of gender and class critique.

EUROPEAN TRADE COMPANIES AND CHRISTIAN MISSIONARY WORK

The establishment of the European trade companies in India began in the early part of the fifteenth century. The Portuguese, the Dutch, the English, and the French vied with each other for trade relations in India. They fought each other through both mercantile and military enterprises. Ultimately, England emerged as the sole colonial power in India.

The European maritime travel enterprises are familiar to most Americans. Vasco da Gama had sailed from Lisbon,

Mughal ruler Akbar founded a new religion which was a synthesis of several religions. Called Din-i-Ilahi, this composite religion was a quest after and an endeavor to seek a formula that would not offend the religious sensibilities of any, but lift up all that is good, beautiful, and true in the major faiths of the world. Though this religion did not flourish for long, Akbar's attempt was a shrewd effort at keeping various religious groups under a benevolent governance.

Portugal on July 8, 1497 and arrived in India with three vessels on May 17, 1498. The aim of Portugal, at least in the initial stages, was to capture the spice trade of India and the East, a game plan for trade monopoly. Soon Portugal's empire-building instincts developed and it began to establish territories and exert colonial power.

Simultaneously, in another facet of this wrinkled chapter of history, a parallel enterprise was growing—Christian missionary work. Early Portuguese traders actually encountered an existing Christian community in Kerala on the west coast of India. This Christian community, the Mar Thoma Church (mentioned previously), functioned more or less as a caste among other castes. According to a Dalit scholar, they did not seek to share the gospel with their neighbors, nor did they have any relations with the Dalits, the so-called untouchables.[2]

Roman Catholic Missionaries

When the Portugese arrived in India, Pope Nicholas V had given half of the world to the Portugese king in a papal bull. With this official document from the Pope, the king sent many missionaries along with his soldiers and merchants. One renowned Roman Catholic missionary who went to India was Francis Xavier. A friend of Ignatius Loyola who founded the Jesuit Order, he dedicated himself early in life to service.

When a demand came from the King of Portugal for ten missionaries to go to India and convert people in the Portuguese possessions, Francis Xavier was chosen to go along with the papal representative. Francis Xavier set sail on April 7, 1541, at the age of thirty-five.

When Xavier reached the Portuguese possession of Goa, he was shocked to see the immoral behavior of the Portuguese community and the ill treatment meted out to the native people. He worked among the Portuguese colonizers as well as the natives under their control in order to bring about a moral revolution. Xavier traveled thousands of miles throughout the country, preaching and converting the people.

THE STORY OF CHRISTIAN MISSION, PROTESTANT OR ROMAN CATHOLIC, HAS TO BE VIEWED ALONGSIDE THE MANY STORIES OF THE PEOPLE. STORIES OF CONQUEST, STORIES OF FAITH, STORIES OF OPPRESSION, STORIES OF HOPE, STORIES OF STRUGGLE, AND STORIES OF TRIUMPHALISM AND SUFFERING LOVE— ALL ARE IMPORTANT.

The Jama Masjid (mosque) in New Delhi, India

India's movement from mercantile economy to colonial economy in itself is a fascinating yet painful study. Fair trade to free trade is a topic of major interest and relevance today since the trends of globalization are, in fact, neo-colonialism at work. Free trade often takes away more than it gives, especially in the case of the poor (chapter 6, pp. 115-119, discusses the issue of globalization, with particular reference to information technology).

On August 15, 1549, he reached Japan, where he converted many to the Roman Catholic faith. His next destination was China, but unfortunately, he died on the island of Sanacian near Canton. Often called the "Great Apostle of the Indies," he was only forty-six when he died.

His entire work in Asia covered a period of only ten years, but he planted the Christian faith in fifty-two countries, preached it across ten thousand miles, and baptized more than one million believers to his faith. Goa in India was the launching pad for all of his work in Asia. His order, the Jesuits, was more dynamic than other Roman Catholic orders in mission to India.[3]

The story of Christian mission, Protestant or Roman Catholic, has to be viewed alongside the many stories of the people. Stories of conquest, stories of faith, stories of oppression, stories of hope, stories of struggle, and stories of triumphalism and suffering love—all are important. The stories of faith, hope, and love will endure, while the stories of triumphalist mission, stories of conquest and forced conversions will be a sore wound in the study of mission history. Mission continued in the name of the spirit of the gospel, in Christ's Way, will win not by might, not by power, but by the power of the Spirit.

Muslims at Badshahi Mosque, Lahore, Pakistan, celebrating EID Day, a day of thanksgiving festivities and rejoicing.

Following the Portuguese pattern, the Dutch rounded the Cape of Hope, challenging Portugal's monopoly of the sea route to the Spice Islands. The Dutch soon consolidated small trading companies and formed the Dutch United East India Company, which monopolized the entire spice trade of the East with Europe. They expanded the number of trade commodities and included cotton goods and other textile products in their commercial venture.

Soon, however, in this relentless game of cutthroat competition, the English ousted the Dutch. In 1600, Queen Elizabeth I of England created the first corporation of London investors in the East India Company. The Queen gave them the monopoly of trade with the East Indies, the territory between Cape of Good Hope and Magellan. Other British companies came into being, such as The Royal African Company, a major slave trading agency, and The Hudson Bay Company, the largest profit-driven, mercantile agency based in North America. Already there were other European companies that had received trade monopolies from their respective national governments. These

Seven Blunders

Wealth without work

Pleasure without conscience

Knowledge without character

Commerce without morality

Science without humanity

Worship without sacrifice

Politics without principles.

—Gandhi

A large number of Indians may not have known the British personally or had daily interactions with them, but they came to associate some products with the British. The glamor of "things British" was something Indians could not resist, just as pop music and blue jeans from the United States are currently much loved by Indian youth. My childhood home in Sri Lanka had a Singer sewing machine made in Great Britain. With due respect, it was brought to India during the ethnic conflict in Sri Lanka. My mother taught me to peddle the old-fashioned foot pedal of the machine when I was a teenager. The shiny British Singer sewing machine was the ultimate skill-building tool a mother could give to her daughter in those days. My mother also used a precious Sheffield knife for slicing bread. She gave the knife to my brother. The imported commodities had such glamor throughout the colonies.

—Glory Dharmaraj

companies were the forerunners of the modern day global corporations ruling vast regions around the world.

During the reign of King James I of England, trade negotiations were going on between England and India. Readers may recall that the King James Version Bible (KJV) was published in 1611 in England. At the same time, diplomatic negotiations were going on in the Indian subcontinent at other levels between the British government and traders and the Indian rulers. King James I sent a royal ambassador, Thomas Roe, with twenty-five thousand pieces of gold and a letter to the ruling king of India, Mughal Emperor Jahangir, whose predecessor built the Taj Mahal.

With more negotiations and more ambassadorial mediations, the British secured trade acquisitions with the Indian ruler over and above other European powers. The British East India Company emerged as the leading consolidating trade power in India. Indian artistry, including its exquisite woven textiles and its jewelry of gold and precious gems, was becoming an important commodity.

The English Parliament passed protective legislation offering subsidiaries and duties for the benefit of the English textile industries. In some instances the mercantile company went to the extent of cutting off the thumbs of Indian weavers of muslin to protect its own colonial economy. Basic commodities like sugar, salt, and cotton, products available and produced for native consumption by local manufacturers, came under the

Muslim market near Char Minar temple, Hyderabad, India

company's governance. The story of cotton is an instance of a trade monopoly as well as a liberation struggle.

At first, the moral corruption of the company's colonies and settlement made it impossible for them to allow Christian missionaries into India. Eventually, however, the Anglican Church of England pressured the British East India Company and the latter was forced to give permission.

Protestant Missionaries

The first Protestant missionaries arrived in India much later than the Catholics. They were Bartholomaeus Ziegenbalg and Henry Plutschau, Germans who came to India in 1706. Sent by a Dutch mission society, they founded what is known as the Tranquebar Mission.

When Bartholomaeus Zieganbalg went to India, he found it difficult to explain who and what a missionary is in a land that had never experienced a missionary presence before. When asked by the local people, "Pray Sir, who and what are you?" Zieganbalg said, "I am minister or servant of the Living God, who created Heaven and Earth, sent to you to warn to leave the idols of your own making, and to turn to the Worship of the true God."[4]

How does it feel to encounter a people who have not imagined you? A world which has not imagined you? Pioneer missionaries worked within this peculiar context. For us, this is a question worth asking and even answering, in the very recent practice of The United Methodist Church's employment of cross-cultural and cross-racial appointments.

Many missionaries from several denominations went to India in the nineteenth century. Among them was William Carey, a Baptist missionary who went to India in 1793. He set up a Bible factory near Calcutta and translated the Bible into more than thirty languages. The majority of these missionaries were evangelicals from Great Britain and the United States. Like the Catholics who preceded them, the Protestant missionaries went to India to evangelize the people.

The East India Company and the Colonial Sword

The great Mogul, Emperor of Hindostan, one of the mightiest Potentates on earth, is become a poor, little, impotent slave to a Company of Merchants! His large, flourishing empire is broken in pieces and covered with fraud, oppression, and misery! And we may call the myriads that have been murdered happy, in comparison with those that still groan under the iron yoke. Wilt thou not visit for these things, O Lord! Shall the fool still say in his heart, 'There is no God?'

—John Wesley
(Journal, Feb. 2, 1776, IV, 68)[5]

Until 1812, no Christian missionary was allowed to stay in the company's colonies or settlements. Moral corruption and trade rules made it impossible for the company to allow even the most innocent Christian influence. The Charter Act of 1813 approved the permanent presence of missionaries. This paved the way for the first Anglican Church of Calcutta. The legalization of English education in 1835 made it possible for the introduction of English schools and universities. Western science and education were introduced as benefits of a higher culture and the primary agents of civilization. Christianization and colonization went hand in hand. The British post-colonial secular press were later to call it the "white man's burden."

We are caught in a destructive system, and we find that even our will to refuse to identify with that system is mixed with the desire to enjoy its fruits. None of us is innocent, either in intention or behavior.

—John B. Cobb, Jr.,
"Christian Existence in a World of Limits"
in *Simpler Living, Compassionate Life: A Christian Perspective.*
Ed. Michael Schut.
(Denver: Earth Ministry, 2001), p. 117.

John C. Goodwin

Mosque in Pakistan

A Story from the Eighteenth Century: Clorinda

The story of Clorinda provides some respite from the linear way of narrating history. It is a story of love played out in the context of colonial mission.

I want to share my personal story with you. I am a Brahmin widow from a royal family. My story reaches back to the mid-eighteenth century. I was married as a child, but my husband died when I was still very young. According to the Hindu custom of those days, I was laid by my dead husband's body to be burnt. This evil practice is called "Sati."

One of the British officers who were watching this cruel practice of burning the widow alive with her husband's dead body saved me from the funeral pyre. You should have seen the anger of my orthodox family. They disowned me. I had no one to turn to. Captain Lyttleton of the British East India Company took me to the military garrison with him. The Hindus hated me because I did not die with my husband. The Christians gossiped because I went with Captain Lyttleton. I did not know this man before, but I had nowhere else to turn. So I followed him.

I lived with Lyttleton, who often suffered from prolonged attacks of gout. I nursed him in this land far from his home until he died. But you know, it was he who introduced me to Christ and to the Christian way of accepting everyone. Captain Lyttleton did not want me to depend on anyone, so he left all his property to me.

My only desire at this point in my life was to spread the gospel to everyone. I sought baptism. Do you remember the date of your baptism? I remembered my day of baptism until my death. It was March 3, 1778.

Now, with this new freedom in Christ, I was able to go into the surrounding villages and spread the gospel. My first list of baptized Christians contains names from all castes, high and low. This is the birth of a new Christian community. I built a church and started a school. The church stands in my memory even today in the southern part of India. I did philanthropic work until I died in my sixtieth year in 1806.

THE STORY OF THE ENFIELD RIFLE

The year was 1857. That year saw the British inauguration of three major universities in India, the Universities of Calcutta, Bombay, and Madras, that were soon to become prestigious secular learning centers of higher education. This was also the year that saw the first uprising of the natives against the British.

The swift fire power of the Enfield rifle was a credit to the British manufacturers of firearms. But the loading of the rifle was characterized by a lack of cultural awareness. The cartridges were filled with animal fat, and British officers gave instructions to native soldiers to bite off the animal fat before inserting the cartridge into the open breech. Thus, the Enfield rifle became a source of a native uprising.

A Dalit rendering of history, so far not much popularized, recounts that a Dalit worker asked a Brahmin soldier, Mangal Pande, for a cup of water from his "lota" (water container). The soldier refused, saying that the Dalit's touch would pollute his vessel. The worker retorted that soon the "Sahib log," the Englishmen, would make everyone bite cartridges dipped in cow and pork fat. He posed a penetrating question: "What would happen to the Brahmin caste then?"

Cows and pigs are sacred and pollutant animals to both Hindus and Muslims. So biting a cartridge dipped in the fat of one of these animals was considered a profane act by both the Hindu and the Muslim soldiers. These soldiers refused to obey the commands of their British officers. When the British officers countered by insisting that the orders be obeyed, the native soldiers revolted against them.

Those who refused to follow the orders of the British were discharged or killed in large numbers. The extensive massacre of Indians that ensued led eventually to the end of the rule of the East India Company. On August 2, 1858, British Parliament transferred the rule of India from the company to the British Crown. Queen Victoria became the full sovereign of India, and both the government and the revenues came directly under her rule.

Historians refer to the 1857 event as the Sepoy Mutiny, or the Soldiers' Mutiny. It is also referred to as the first struggle of independence by the writers of the underside of history, post-colonial historians.

THE STORY OF COTTON

The movement of imported goods from one place to the other within India had been made possible as early as the 1850s by the construction of railways. Mumbai (Bombay) in the West, Delhi in the central north, and Kolkotha (Calcutta) in the East were connected by a huge network of railway lines.

Coal and cotton, raw materials for the industrialization of British economy, were moved easily from one center to the other and then on to England. Raw cotton from India was transported to cotton mills in Manchester. Until the American Civil War, the Manchester mills relied on the United States for its cotton. After 1860, Manchester and Lancaster turned to India for raw cotton. The finished product was sold back to the colonized countries, including India.

The boycott of British goods was launched in India at the turn of the twentieth century as a movement to resist British rule. People vowed not to buy British produced cloth, salt, sugar, and manufactured goods. This was called the "Swedeshi" (**swe DAI shi**) movement, the struggle for "one's own country." The movement went beyond industry to include other arenas such as art, culture, literature, and so forth.

In his later life, Gandhi took up spinning yarn on a spinning wheel, a major symbol of his statement against the exploitation of the colonial economy. In large numbers, people threw British-made clothing onto fires. Protests using such bonfires spread across the country. People began wearing clothes of cotton spun on native wheels and woven in native factories. Wearing "Khadi" (**KAA di**), homespun cotton, became a symbol of resistance.

THE STORY OF SALT

Something else which triggered non-violent revolt was the levying of a heavy tax on salt. In India, the British government had a monopoly on the production of this essential commodity. Even a person who lived near the sea and picked up natural salt could be arrested under the law.

Gandhi rallied the masses around the issue of salt and led what came to be known as the Salt March. On March 12, 1930, he led a group of people who were dedicated to non-violence. By this time, Gandhi, a British-trained lawyer, had given up his western dress, and covered himself from his knees up to his waist with a cloth called a dhoti. As a symbol of his solidarity with the poorest of the poor, he did not even wear a shirt.

A pilgrim leading his people into one more defiant act of civil disobedience, Gandhi's march mobilized more and more people on the march. He walked from a beach into the waters and picked up a lump of salt. Women joined the march led by Sarojini Naidu (**Sa roo jini Naa yu du**). When she joined the pilgrims led by Gandhi, she shouted, "Hail, law breaker!" A simple pan was set up by the sea to manufacture salt. Gandhi issued a public statement encouraging people across the country to make salt in their own areas or to redeem salt from the seas.

Gandhi's Salt March initiated a full-blown Civil Disobedience Movement. Peaceful picketing, non-violent strikes, resignation from government jobs, and refusal to join the military were some of the aspects of the movement. Many thousands offered themselves to be arrested with no retaliation to police brutality. A great Muslim leader, Khan Abdul Ghaffar Khan, from the North-West Frontier Province in what is today's Pakistan, participated in this movement with his followers. He came to be called "Frontier Gandhi," a symbol of Muslim peaceful resistance.

Gandhi conveyed deep spiritual ideas through politics. He used Satyagraha (**sat yaa gra HAA**), literally, "firm grasp of the truth," as a moral weapon. His early law practice in racially divided South Africa had motivated him to undertake this moral and spiritual journey. He knew that the colonized did not stand a chance of defeating an empire without moral strength. He used "Ahimsa" (**a him SAA**), non-violence, another moral technique. Converting moral virtues into ethical and spiritual techniques for national liberation is Gandhi's contribution to world peace. Later, Martin Luther King, Jr., followed the footsteps of Gandhi.

LINKS FROM GANDHI TO U.S. CIVIL RIGHTS

What is not often known is the link forged between the Gandhian movement in India and the Civil Rights Movement in the U.S. by the then Woman's Division of the Board of Global Ministries. At that time, James Lawson was a student at Vanderbilt School of Theology in Nashville, Tennessee. A Methodist, Lawson was a leader in the Methodist Youth Fellowship at the national level. His clarion call for equality was galvanizing Methodist youth across the country.

In a strategic time, in a strategic place, the Woman's Division invested once again in a youth leader. Thelma Stevens, then a staff person from Mississippi engaged in racial justice, arranged for the Woman's Division to send Lawson for three years "as a missionary to India to study Gandhi's movement, teachings, and methods for non-violent change."

Lawson's leadership with the Methodist Youth Federation and the Fellowship of Reconciliation, an organization dedicated in the 1950s and 1960s to addressing racial segregation by non-violent means, is known to history. His name is cited in the Civil Rights Museum of Birmingham, Alabama, as someone who studied Gandhian methods.

But what is left unsaid in that museum display is the Woman's Division's role in it, especially, the role of Thelma Stevens.[6]

THE CONVERSION OF KING ASHOKA

Becoming a king some time around 269–268 BCE, Ashoka, whose name means "sorrow free," had the ambition to become an emperor by expanding his kingdom. The strategic and cruel war which he fought during his reign was over Kalinga (**Ka LING gaa**), the modern day state of Orissa in India. During the war, 150,000 persons were deported and many times that number perished.

After the war, Ashoka felt remorse and underwent a deep conversion experience. He embraced Buddhism. By his command, the records of his repentance were inscribed on a rock, along with the havoc he had earlier caused. Writings on stones and rocks were a means of memorializing one's moral and political legacies. Known as a rock edict, this royal decree is a standing testimony for posterity. Ashoka also wrote:

> Today if a hundredth or a thousandth part of those people who were killed or died or were deported when Kalinga was annexed were to suffer similarly, it would weigh heavily on the mind of the Beloved of the Gods.[7]

True conquest was not by arms, he decided, but by piety and virtue. There are a number of rock edicts remaining that carry the public record of his commands, deeds, and propagation.

Ashoka instructed his son and daughter through a public policy of waging peace. He sent his son, Mahendra (**ma HEIND ra**), and daughter, Sangamitra (**san ga MITH ra**), as missionaries to Sri Lanka to propagate Buddhism. Ashoka himself went on religious pilgrimages and spent the rest of his rule in propagating mutual good will and peace. Tolerant of other religions in a multireligious country, Ashoka touched the deep religious psyche of India for the power and potential of peace and non-violence. For him, this was a strategy for true liberation of a national community.

Kashmir is famous for its natural beauty and has often been referred to as the "Switzerland of the East."

3

KASHMIR: BONE OF CONTENTION

IT'S A CHALLENGE
TO BE IN THE MAJORITY
GRACEFULLY AND
TO BE IN THE MINORITY
GRACIOUSLY.

—GEORGE NIEDERAUER,
THE NEW YORK TIMES,
JANUARY 20, 2002.

Within the multiplicity of religions and cultures on the subcontinent is a destructive struggle between two major religious and political entities, Hindus and Muslims. This is sometimes felt as the tremors of a subterranean fuel, and sometimes manifested as an explosive molten lava flowing from a heretofore contained volcano. Independence from the British rule was granted to Pakistan on August 14, 1947. A day later, India was independent. Pakistan for majority Muslims and India for majority Hindus was the vision for the subcontinent, yet the best laid plans for a secular, united India failed. This chapter examines the religio-political bone of contention between India and Pakistan: Kashmir.

As the British troopships pulled away to the familiar tunes of "Auld Lang Syne," Gurkhas, Sikhs, Marathas, Hindus, Muslims, and Christians all sang. They were part of a multicultural, multireligious, and multinational band called India. However, there were seething cauldrons of separatist tendencies ready to boil over. An outbreak of unchecked ethnic reactionary flash floods occurred. The price of independence has been costly for both countries. At the awakening of independence, two million people died and eleven million became refugees. Ethnic cleansing ran rampant, and Gandhi went on an indefinite fast.

The impact of partition left its mark on Christian mission, too. Christians in Pakistan and India were divided by the political border line, the Body of Christ artificially divided by the scalpels of history. Forman Christian College, an institution supported by Presbyterians and Methodists in Lahore, Punjab, suffered the impact of partition. Many students were Muslims; the majority of staff were Hindus and Sikhs. Partition's scalpel drove them in great numbers either to Pakistan or to India, based on their religious affiliation.

Nevertheless, Christian mission, with its healing work, rose to the occasion. Soon afterwards, the college opened its doors to emergency relief.[1] Christians on both sides of the border worked tirelessly for the refugees fleeing into Pakistan. It was the birth of United Christian Hospital in Lahore, Pakistan, a product of the partition. The General Board of Global Ministries of The United Methodist Church had its missionaries in this hospital until the 1990s. The Board continues to support this medical mission in the latter's new branches of a public health department and immunization and prenatal care, with the hospital's national medical director at the helm. Now the hospital has about seventy-five beds.

During the partition in 1947, Gandhi's was a radical and daring voice of love. In the midst of hatred and tragedy, against the backdrop of refugees fleeing by the millions, against the noise and silence of killings and rapes, Gandhi embarked on a quest of healing and stability. He went on an indefinite fast. A steady moral and spiritual voice in a shaky body politic, he protested the ethnic cleansing of Muslims in India. Gandhi, a Hindu by birth, stood in solidarity with the minority Muslim population in India. He paid the ultimate price: death in 1948 at the hands of a Hindu fanatic, Nathuram Godse.

E. Stanley Jones, a Methodist missionary from the U.S. to India and a long-time friend of Gandhi, commented that Gandhi had laid the cross of Jesus the Christ across the political life of

Kashmir:
The Metaphor of the Cruel Game

*A medieval woman born in Kashmir, Padmavathi (**pad maa vaa thi**), was caught in the cruel game of an oppressive mother-in-law and a willing husband who became part of the oppressor's game. One morning, she decided to leave this time-sanctioned game of arranged marriage to her mother-in-law and her husband. She abandoned them both to their schemes of domestic politics.*

She renounced her home and became a reformer who questioned the religious systems that make people subservient. In the language of the Kashmiri people, in their own idiom, she spoke against the barriers imposed by religions. She sang her protest and called for a unity beyond the narrow divisions imposed by Hinduism and Islam.

India. Gandhi dared the impossible, practicing hitherto unheard of ideals of peace and non-violence in the midst of a festering body of homegrown ethnic conflicts set within the arena of international politics. Gandhi's practice of non-violence as a political strategy is still a challenge to those who believe in violence and militarism as a means of solving conflicts.

NEW INDIA AND NEW PAKISTAN

Today, the new India and new Pakistan exist as countries forged from conflict and subject to its legacy. The Islamic Republic of Pakistan, with Islamabad as its capital, has four provinces: the Punjab, Sindh, Baluchistan, and North West Frontier Province. The Northern areas bordering China and Afghanistan are also federally administered by Pakistan. Ninety-six percent of the people of Pakistan are Muslims, about 3 percent are Christians, and 1 percent other minorities. India, with some twenty-seven states and six Union Territories, has as its capital New Delhi. Hindus are a majority in India. About 3 percent of India's population are Christians.

Kashmir emerged as the bone of contention in partition politics in 1947. The notion of Pakistan as a separate nation came into existence at a later stage in the long struggle of India against British imperialism. Kashmir does not fit into a neat analysis of history. The story of Kashmir should be examined in the context of the struggle for India's independence.

Deep Roots of Partition

Two of the forces leading to the partition of India are theocracy and democracy. This led to the establishment of both the Islamic state of Pakistan and the secular state of India. In 1885, the Indian National Congress was founded. Participants were mostly graduates of the universities founded by the British in 1857 in Kolkotha (Calcutta), Mumbai (Bombay), and Chennai (Madras), and they worked on reforms and requested the representation of Indians in the British civil services.

This is the native spirit of Kashmir: an oppressed woman taking charge of her own destiny and speaking to the Kashmiri masses in their own Kashmiri language, not in the language of Hindus or Muslims. It is the essence of Kashmir: a spirit of suffering—love triumphing over the narrow confines of alien powers trying to determine her destiny.

Maybe the international community is waiting and asking the real Kashmir to stand up and to speak out for herself. Not India or Pakistan! Will the mother-in-law and the husband stand aside, please? Kashmir, as in the case of Padmavathi, an emancipated woman who has suffered enough, has to be seen beyond the arranged marriage of political alliances. Kashmir must be seen in its own selfhood.

Within the Indian National Congress there emerged a second stream of national consciousness. It called for the return to the "golden age" of Hinduism. This rift in the India National Congress became stronger, one side consisting of extremists and users of religious revivals with recourse to force, the other side standing for moderates and secularists, who demanded freedom without recourse to force.

A further addition was the emergence of the Muslim consciousness. Some Muslim leaders felt that the Indian National Congress was a Hindu organization. So the Muslim League was founded in 1906.

During World War I, both organizations, the Indian National Congress and the Muslim League, expressed a common desire for freedom from colonial rule, yet demonstrated loyalty to the British in the war. In fact, a million Indian volunteers were enlisted in the British army. The Indian army took the brunt of casualties in the Middle East and east Africa. The British rulers made a wartime promise to give freedom to India, only to completely forget this promise in the time of peace that followed World War I.

Together, the Indian National Congress and the Muslim League devised what is known as the Lucknow Pact in 1916, which marked the formal acceptance of a separate electorate for Muslims. National independence was a joint goal. Hindu-Muslim unity was a given. When the British rulers did not heed either India's call for freedom or for the territorial preservation of Turkey, Muslims in India issued what is known as the Khilafat Manifesto. It was both a call for nationalism and an expression of pan-Islamic solidarity.

Though there were some secular voices within the Muslim League, the simultaneous goals of Muslim autonomy and freedom from the British became a rallying point around which the members of the Muslim League began to operate. Hindu-Muslim unity in the cause of an undivided nation became elusive. Religion became a focal point and a founding principle of the future nation state, Pakistan.

THE BRITISH RULERS MADE A WARTIME PROMISE TO GIVE FREEDOM TO INDIA, ONLY TO COMPLETELY FORGET THIS PROMISE IN THE TIME OF PEACE THAT FOLLOWED WORLD WAR I.

The Laxmi Narayan Mandir Temple in Jaipur, India, built by B. D. Birla, is a modern Hindu temple dedicated to Laxmi, the goddess of Wealth, and Narayana, the preserver. Inaugurated by Gandhi, it is open to all castes (including the Dalits) and all faiths.

**Pakistan—
A Consolidated Nation State:**

    Punjab,

    Afghan Province,

    Kashmir,

    Sindh, and

Baluchis TAN

In 1933, the notion of a separate Muslim nation became more pronounced. Some of the Muslim students in Cambridge University in England coined the name Pakistan. Their vision was of a consolidated nation state created from **P**unjab, **A**fghan Province, **K**ashmir, **S**indh, and Baluchis**TAN**.[2]

The Pakistan concept further evolved when in 1940 the Muslim League produced a resolution in Lahore for the partition of India along religious and confessional lines—that is, along majority Hindu and Muslim groupings of constituents. Those dividing lines would not be cut incisively sharply and impeccably neatly by the knife of partition. Historic wounds from historic mistakes would fester and bleed, beckoning Indians of every background to be more than bystanders. To complicate matters further, there were the Sikhs, born and raised in the Punjab, where the knife of the coming partition would cut deeply.

In 1944, Muhammed Ali Jinnah, a barrister trained in England and later the first Governor General of the future

Pakistan, pressed for the establishment of West and East Pakistan. In the earlier years, he had been close to some of the moderates in the Indian National Congress. The Congress continued to struggle to maintain an undivided India.

A Princely Procrastination

In this complex mix called the Indian subcontinent, there were also 570 so-called princely states. The British had the princes under their rule, offering them the veneer of sovereignty, pomp, and pride as kings in their own little kingdoms, while the British actually ruled over them in a vast empire "where the sun never set." When independence came, these princes had to make a decision to cast their lot either with the future India or with Pakistan by sunset on the evening of August 15, 1947.

Three princely states did not fall neatly under either the Hindu or the Muslim majority groupings under their respective religious leaders. One of the three was Kashmir, ruled by a Maharaja, a Hindu whose majority subjects were Muslims. Another was Hyderabad, ruled by a Muslim whose majority subjects were Hindus. The third, Junagadh, was ruled by a Muslim whose majority were Hindus. On the eve of the forthcoming partition, the complexity of these aforesaid three states was not resolved. So the princes merely postponed their decision.

In 1947, West and East Pakistan were created as a nation-state based on religion. Kashmir had about four million people, three-fourths of them Muslim. It had an area of 84,471 square miles divided into five distinct areas: the Vale of Kashmir, Jammu, Ladakh, Balistan, and Poonch and Gilgit.

With neither the will to join Pakistan under Islam nor India under democracy, the prince of Kashmir postponed his decision. His procrastination proved to be costly. India adopted a secular constitution. Pakistan sought to follow "the principles of democracy, freedom, equality, tolerance, and social justice as enunciated by Islam,"[3] and became an Islamic state.

Pakistan sought to follow "the principles of democracy, freedom, equality, tolerance, and social justice as enunciated by Islam,"[3] and became an Islamic state.

> *The British East India Company sold Kashmir to Gulab Singh for a million and a half dollars — a mere pittance.*

History of Kashmir

From the third century BCE to the fourteenth century CE, Kashmir was ruled by Buddhist and Hindu rulers. In the fourteenth century, Rinchin, a Tibetan soldier and a Buddhist, came to power. He embraced Islam and became the first Muslim ruler of Kashmir. Muslims ruled until 1819 when Ranjit Singh, a Sikh ruler, conquered Kashmir.

In 1846, the British East India Company placed Kashmir under the control of the Dogra-Hindu dynasty. Gulab Singh, a strategist and an opportunist, helped the British in the transfer of power from the Sikhs. The British East India Company sold Kashmir to Gulab Singh for a million and a half dollars—a mere pittance. The ruler was the owner of Kashmir until the 1930s. Non-Dogras and Muslims were excluded from Civil Service until the 1930s.

Status of Forces in Kashmir at the Partition

Sheikh Muhammad Abdullah, a Muslim and a native of Kashmir, who was later called the "Lion of Kashmir," founded the All-Jammu and Kashmir Muslim Conference in 1932, demanding the representation of Muslims in the civil rule of the state. Gradually, the All-Jammu and Kashmir Muslim Conference became an inclusive organization moving beyond its inception as solely a Muslim organization. This political party called itself the All-Jammu and Kashmir National Conference.

Some Muslims were disenchanted with this inclusive model and went back to the early days of the National Conference, reviving it as a Muslim conference. Choudhry Ghulam Abbas, a leader of the Muslim conference, wanted Kashmir to join Pakistan. But Sheikh Abdullah, a leader of the All-Jammu and Kashmir National Conference, stood firm on a multicultural and secular ideal for Kashmir within India. The Hindu ruler of Kashmir, Hari Singh, wanted an independent Kashmir to preserve his throne.

Pakistani mosque

Sir Cyril Radcliffe...helped run a scalpel along religious lines dividing West and East Pakistan from mainland India. The partition lines also ran through Kashmir.

June 1947 was the time slated for the partition. Sir Cyril Radcliffe, the British official charged with working with the Boundary Commission to determine the shape of the partition, helped run a scalpel along religious lines dividing West and East Pakistan from mainland India. The partition lines also ran through Kashmir.

The Hindu ruler of Kashmir, Hari Singh, signed "standstill agreements" with the newly independent India and Pakistan, since he could not decide to join either Pakistan or India. One could only guess that he might have envisioned a country independent of either of the neighboring nations. With the religious and ethnic composition of its inhabitants, this was not to be Kashmir's destiny. A bloodier path to an elusive peace was to be the fate of this paradise on earth.

Kashmir as Battleground

Pakistan and India both gained independence in August of 1947. In October 1947, the chieftains and tribal men of Pakistan's North West Frontier Province went on the attack to "liberate" Kashmir in the name of Islam from the "Hindu Raj" and to celebrate the Muslim festival of Id in the mosque of Srinagar, the capital of Jammu-Kashmir. India called it an "invasion." Pakistan denied its support of the tribal men in their attack. The war that ensued between India and Pakistan continued for fifteen months.

Pakistan and India both gained independence in August of 1947.

In the meantime, on October 26, 1947, Hari Singh, the Hindu ruler of Kashmir, acceded formally to India. Sheikh Abdullah became the head of the administration of Kashmir. But the undeclared war over Kashmir continued between Pakistan and India.

Lord Louis Mountbatten, the first Governor General of the new India by the good will of the people of India, declared that the Indian government, while accepting the accession of Kashmir by Hari Singh, wanted the issue of accession settled by the people of Kashmir, once her soil was cleared of the invader. The same sentiment was echoed by Sheikh Abdullah when he sent a message to Pakistan asking Jinnah to accept the "democratic principle of the sovereignty of people" of the Kashmiri people.

In short, "plebiscite" was the concept put forward by both the popular leader of Kashmir, Sheikh Abdullah, and Lord Mountbattan, the first Governor General of India, backed by Jawaharlal Nehru, the first Prime Minister of India. Nehru made his stance public when he said that once law and order was restored in Kashmir, he promised that a U.N.-supervised plebiscite would take place.

The U.N. Security Council organized a cease fire and a line of control on January 1, 1949, drawing the boundary lines between the Indian-held area and the Pakistani-held area. Kashmir, too, was partitioned. The area under the control of Pakistan came to be known as "Azad Kashmir," free Kashmir, by Pakistan. The Muslim Conference moved to Pakistan-controlled Kashmir.

Indian-controlled Kashmir received a "special status" from the Indian government. Because Sheikh Abdullah and his government were in the area controlled by India, he became the Chief Minister of the new "state." If Sheikh Abdullah's original vision had been to join Pakistan, things would have been much easier. However, he was a secular Muslim who believed in the ideals of Gandhi and Nehru, who were themselves steering the new India clear of possible Hindu fundamentalism (extremism), thus assuring a secular constitution for India's religious minorities.

On April 21, 1949, the U.N. Security Council Resolution introduced some key actions: (1) That the Government of Pakistan should clear Kashmir of "tribesmen and Pakistani nationals" who were there for the "purposes of fighting" and stop "furnishing of material aid to those fighting" in Kashmir. (2) That the Government of India should work for a "Plebiscite Administration in Kashmir" once the "tribesmen" withdrew. (3) That when the cessation of the fighting had become effective, India and Pakistan reduce their forces from Jammu and Kashmir. Pakistan refused to implement its mandate; India refused its mandate from the U.N.; the Kashmir issue was internationalized.

Another cease fire effort by the U.N. came on September 23, 1965. In 1971, India helped East Pakistan to become a free country under a new name, Bangla Desh. The emergence of this new country was a loss to Pakistan. India and Pakistan agreed to respect the Jammu and Kashmir "line of control" resulting from the cease fire of December 17, 1971, and to solve the problem through "bilateral negotiations." This is the essence of what is known as the Simla Agreement in the summer of 1972 between Pakistan and India.[4]

THE COLD WAR AND ITS IMPACT ON THE REGION

Kashmir is a militarily strategic location. Its northern border touches three countries; the former Soviet Union, China, and Afghanistan. In the ensuing political stalemate, the two superpowers of the time (the United States and the U.S.S.R.) attempted to influence Pakistan and India.

Pakistan received support and arms from the United States. In spite of its status as a Non-Aligned Nation, India leaned on the former Soviet Union. Pakistan and India were caught in their own ambitions to retain Kashmir as a strategic geopolitical site. They were also enmeshed in the cold war struggle, a power game between two superpowers. In 1979, the Soviet

On April 21, 1949, the U.N. Security Council Resolution introduced some key actions:

1 That the Government of Pakistan should clear Kashmir of "tribesmen and Pakistani nationals" who were there for the "purposes of fighting" and stop "furnishing of material aid to those fighting" in Kashmir.

2 That the Government of India should work for a "Plebiscite Administration in Kashmir" once the "tribesmen" withdrew.

3 That when the cessation of the fighting had become effective, India and Pakistan should reduce their forces from Jammu and Kashmir.

Others have their message. I have another message— for those who have suffered from love speak another language.[5]

— *Sheikh Abdullah*

Union invaded Afghanistan in order to support its government against the Mujahideen, who united under the name of Islam against the former Soviet Union. The United States sent military and intelligence support to these "freedom fighters." This support was mostly channeled through Pakistan.

By the end of the 1980s, the United States was sending more than 65,000 tons of arms annually to the Mujahideen. Between 1980-1985, the C.I.A. funded the recruitment and training of many volunteers from other Muslim countries to fight the Soviet Union in Afghanistan. The latter's use of Stinger anti-aircraft missiles helped ward off Soviet Union control over Afghanistan in 1989. Funds were received by the Mujahideen from Saudi Arabia and the gulf Arab states. Among those who came to fight for Afghanistan was Osama bin Laden, heir to a Saudi construction fortune.

The Taliban, which literally means "students" in the Peshtu language, became a recognizable force in 1993. Many were trained in religious schools in Pakistan and followed an extremist interpretation of Islam. In 1999, U.N. Security Council Resolution 1267 imposed economic sanctions on Afghanistan for offering shelter to Osama bin Laden, who by this time was linked with Al Qaeda and its terrorist acts.

Extremist Islamic Forces in Kashmir

Sheikh Abdullah, the popular leader of Kashmir who had negotiated a special status for Kashmir with India, kept clear of extremist elements. After his death in 1982, things began to change. While a movement such as the Jammu and Kashmir Liberation Front demanded secular nationalism and total independence from both India and Pakistan, extremist Islamist groups like Jama'at-i-Islami and Hizbul Mujahideen were also emerging. These extremist groups view the struggle for Kashmir as Jihad, a holy war—Islam against all non-believers. The Jammu and Kashmir Liberation Front has continued to stand for an independent Kashmir that would be made up of the areas currently controlled by India, Pakistan, and China.

Extremist Islamist groups believed that the mainline followers of Islam in Kashmir were not devout enough in the practice of their faith. Hardline Islamists with recourse to violence took center stage. Currently, the Lashkar-e-Toiba (whose name was changed after September 11, 2001, to Pasban-e-Ahle-Hadith) and Jaish-e-Mohammad are two such groups. The Taliban and Al Qaeda forces are set against a secular nationalist Kashmir otherwise known as "Kashmiriyat," a vision lifted up by the secular Jammu and Kashmir Liberation Front. Kashmiriyat, which includes religious freedom, is the essence of Kashmir.

India had begun conducting underground nuclear tests in 1974, then conducted above ground nuclear weapons tests in 1998. Pakistan also tested its nuclear weapons. Aghast, the rest of the world watched this deadly competition. Faith communities spoke out.[6] Sanctions were imposed by the United States.

After September 11, 2001

September 11, 2001 saw the tragic attack on the World Trade Center in New York City and the Pentagon in Washington, D.C. The connection between Al Qaeda and the attack has been established, as has the connection between Al Qaeda and militant Kashmiri groups such as the Jaish-e-Mohammad.

"One hundred and twenty-two billion dollars have been spent on Theater and National Missile Defense since World War II. Furthermore, the Pentagon believes that it would cost the American people $26.6 billion to maintain a single missile defense site in Alaska, with $4 billion in annual maintenance fees. Each ballistic missile test conducted by the U.S. has cost over $100 million, mostly resulting in waste. In total, the U.S. has spent $5.6 trillion in nuclear arsenals. In fact, if all the dollars spent on nuclear weapons since 1945 were stacked one on top of another, it would reach the moon and almost back again."[7]

United Christian Hospital in Lahore, Pakistan

John C. Goodwin

Total Number of Nuclear Weapons Tests

U.S.: **1030**

Russia: **715**

France: **210**

China: **45**

U.K.: **45**

India: **6**

Pakistan: **6**[8]

In the current geopolitical context, the United States has found itself in a situation in which its old ally, Pakistan, as well as its new friend, India, are both needed for an aggressive peace.

The sanctions imposed on both countries due to their nuclear weapons testing in the late 1990s had to be lifted, since Pakistan's role in fighting the War Against Terror was crucial. President General Pervez Musharraf of Pakistan took great risks, both personal and political, in his fight against terrorists in Afghanistan for which he won the appreciation of the international community. The second in command in Al Qaeda has called for the overthrow of President Musharraf for his supposed betrayal of Islam.

In the current geopolitical context, the United States has found itself in a situation in which its old ally, Pakistan, as well as its new friend, India, are both needed for an aggressive peace.

Because of the Summit of the South Asian Association for Regional Cooperation in January 2004, communication between Pakistan and India has improved. Former Prime Minister Atal Bihari Vajpayee of India and President Pervez Mushaaraf of Pakistan acknowledged their support to eradicate terrorists in Kashmir.

Neither of these countries can take diplomatic credit for their recent stances, though they have come a long way. The pressure of the United States is the main factor. A lasting and durable peace goes a long way. In the meantime, the United Nations Peacekeeping Forces do their work in Kashmir.[9]

Nuclear Weapons

Nine countries are known to have produced nuclear weapons: Great Britain, China, France, India, Israel, Pakistan, Russia, South Africa, and the United States. More than forty countries have the technical know-how to produce these weapons.[10]

The Treaty on the Non-Proliferation of Nuclear Weapons is critical to the security and stability of the world. Especially after September 11, 2001, the necessity of compliance with major treaties to save the stability of the world is vital. The 106 countries that are parties to the Treaty on the Non-Proliferation of Nuclear Weapons met in Geneva for the April–May 2003 Preparatory Committee. Its purpose was the 2005 Review

Conference of the Parties to the Treaty on the Non-Proliferation of Nuclear Weapons. Since then, India and Pakistan still have not signed the Comprehensive Nuclear Test Ban Treaty. The United States has signed the treaty, but has not ratified it. The withdrawal of the U.S. from the Anti-Ballistic Missile Treaty and its decision to further develop missile defense systems are issues of concern at tables of peace talks on nuclear disarmament and non-proliferation.[11]

Involvement and engagement in creating a nuclear-free world must be pursued. In India, the Institute of Total Revolution, the Movement in India for Nuclear Disarmament (MIND), the Lokayan, and the Pakistan-India People's Forum for Peace and Democracy are some of the efforts at peace. In Pakistan, the Citizen's Peace Committee and the Pakistan Doctors for Peace and Development work towards nuclear disarmament.

An Indian soldier stands guard outside his post along the Line of Control, which separates Kashmir between India and Pakistan, at Baraf Post, 102 miles north of Srinagar, December 2003.

Community health workers at Comprehensive Rural Health Program training session in Jamkhed, India.

4

PEOPLE AT THE MARGINS

It was 1854. Alexander Duff, a Scottish missionary familiar with Christian mission work in India, visited the General Conference of the Methodist Episcopal Church in the U.S., the largest Protestant denomination at that time, and appealed to American Methodists to open mission institutions in India.

Two years later in 1856, William Butler, his wife Clementina, and their four children left for India. Butler went with a dream and a plan of having twenty-five missionaries in six central and a few outlying stations. In 1857, the Butlers started a Methodist Church in a place called Bareilly. The eight original members were Butler and his wife Clementina, Joel Janvier (whom the Butlers picked up from the American Presbyterian Mission from Allahabad), his wife, Ann Hodgkinson, Maria Bolst, (an Anglo-Indian girl who had studied in the Baptist Mission School in Calcutta, and who had gone back to her mother's people in Bareilly), one Isaac, and Palwan. It was Maria, called the first indigenous member of the Methodist Church, who urged the Butlers to go to Bareilly.

In the same year (1857), what is known as the First War of

Independence broke out in India (in Chapter 2, this native uprising against the British is referred to as "The Story of the Enfield Rifle"). A British colonel sent word to the Butlers through a personal messenger urging the missionary family to flee to Naini Tal at the foothills of the Himalayas. Escaping to this place, Butler was able to preach "the first Methodist sermons ever uttered on the Himalayan Mountains." [1]

Meanwhile, Butler's native flock in Bareilly stood firm in its new-found faith under the leadership of Joel Janvier, who preached from the text, "Fear not, little flock." By the close of the prayers, the women were hiding in fear of the soldiers. A soldier saw Maria Bolst running through the trees. Since the soldiers perceived these natives as tools of the imperialist government, one of the soldiers struck Maria with his sword and killed her. She was buried under the rose hedge where she used to sit with Clementina Butler.[2] Maria, "the first female convert of the fledgling mission,"[3] was also the first Methodist woman martyr in India.

EDUCATION OF THE GIRL CHILD IN THE SUBCONTINENT

William Butler asked an Indian gentleman who knew English to teach the girls in India. He replied, "You are going to teach women to read? You will teach the cows next."[4] Duff himself had misgivings about educating Indian girls. He said, "You might as

Students on the steps of Methodist girls' school in Uttar Pradesh, India.

Sarla E. Chand

> *Education of the girl child in the subcontinent had its genesis in the mission schools and colleges founded in the nineteenth century.*

well try to scale a wall thirty yards high as to try to teach an Indian woman to read."[5] But "herstories" soon to follow in Christian mission proved otherwise. Education of the girl child in the subcontinent had its genesis in the mission schools and colleges founded in the nineteenth century.

In South Asia today, more than half of all adults who are illiterate are women. In a society where there is no social security in old age, the prevalent gender perception is that investing in a girl child's education is a waste since the girl has to be married off and will not be of financial benefit to her parents in their old age.

In Pakistan, girls make up 62 percent of the enrollment in primary education. The adult female literacy rate is 25 percent, while the literacy rate for males is 55 percent. In India the literacy rate for males is 64 percent and for females, 35 percent. The average number of years of schooling a girl child receives is less than one year. Two major factors are low parental expectation and limited access to a universal primary education.[6] A girl child's education, then, is placed against enormous odds from start to finish.

But there are signs of hope for the women of India and Pakistan. The Allama Iqbal Open University in Pakistan teaches using distance learning. Between 1998 and 1999, 53 percent of those enrolled in distance higher education were women. This is much higher than the proportion of women attending regular universities, since distance education takes place through correspondence without requiring physical attendance throughout the academic year. Often barriers of distance and financial constraints are hurdles which can be overcome.[7]

COLLEGES FOR WOMEN

Isabella Thoburn College

American women went as missionaries to India beginning in the latter part of the nineteenth century. Congregationist Women began their Woman's Union Missionary Society in 1860. In

Isabella Thoburn College, Lucknow, India

1869, the Woman's Foreign Missionary Society of the Methodist Episcopal Church was the next to organize. Key leaders were Clementina Butler and Mrs. Edwin Parker, both missionary spouses from India, and six other women. When some members "counseled prudence" in finance in their deliberations over sending the first single female missionaries, Mrs. E. P. Porter stood up and delivered the following historic speech:

> Shall we lose Miss Thoburn because we have not the needed money in our hands to send her? No! Rather let us walk the streets of Boston in calico dresses, if need be, and save the expense of more costly apparel! I move the appointment of Miss Thoburn.[8]

Isabella Thoburn's goal was to offer a first-class education to the daughters of native Christians. With just six female students, she opened a school in 1870 that was soon to become a college. The founder of the first college for women in Asia, Thoburn would often say, "No people would ever rise higher, as a people, than the point to which they elevate their women."[9] The college's motto is "We receive to give."

Isabella Thoburn College was the first Christian college for women in India, with a full staff of women and a resident facility for women. It was also the first college to establish a master's

Isabella Thoburn College was the first Christian college for women in India, with a full staff of women and a resident facility for women.

program in Women's Studies.[10] Dr. Sunita Charles, principal of the college, says the "major achievement" has been "to break the silence so that women can talk with each other and realize that issues called women's issues do exist." [11]

As for the Christian witness of the college today, 60 percent of the college's three thousand students come from religious backgrounds other than Christianity. It is a multifaith institution which seeks to broaden the perspectives of the Christian students. Dr. Charles says of the college:

> It enables Christian students to interact with women of other faiths and generates a feeling of security among women of all faiths, which enables them to understand, admire, and appreciate other religions and still practice their own.[12]

College chapel services are a means of sharing with women of other faiths the "meaning of Christianity" and "a living faith which has no closed boundaries."[13]

Kinnaird College for Women

Kinnaird College for Women has pioneered women's higher education in the Punjab in Pakistan since 1913. This Christian college for women is a product of ecumenical mission efforts. By 1956, the Woman's Division of Christian Service had four women on the staff of this college.[14]

Currently the college serves more than twenty-five hundred students, the majority of whom are Muslim women, with 10 percent Christian. Since 2000, seventy-five Christian students have received scholarship grants from the Women's Division. The Christian student population has increased over the years.

Dr. Mira Phailbus, former principal of Kinnaird College who served from 1972 and retired recently, says, "Some Muslims have never seen a Christian. Kinnaird College gives the only opportunity for such a blending. The cream of the society of Muslims and the poorest of the poor rub shoulders here." [15]

Christians who are poor economically are "doubly marginalized," according to Phailbus, for they are "the servants of the

"SOME MUSLIMS HAVE NEVER SEEN A CHRISTIAN. KINNAIRD COLLEGE GIVES THE ONLY OPPORTUNITY FOR SUCH A BLENDING. THE CREAM OF THE SOCIETY OF MUSLIMS AND THE POOREST OF THE POOR RUB SHOULDERS HERE."

Kinnaird College for Women, Lahore, Pakistan

servants." Because they are minority Christians, they are not given opportunities in society. Kinnaird gives opportunities to such Christian women. "Whether Muslim or Christian, if you get to Kinnaird, it is a passport to success." [16]

Phailbus says, with much pride, that most of her students have entered fields such as aviation, law, and human rights activism. This was unimaginable twenty-five years ago when women only studied academic traditional fields such as education and medicine. Of seventy-two members in the Pakistan General Assembly, fourteen are alumnae of Kinnaird College.

After thirty-two years of service, Phailbus retired recently. Kinnard College for Women in Pakistan has a new principal. She is Dr. Ira Hasan. Principal Hasan, former Associate Professor and Head of the Post Graduate Program at Kinnaird, is a widely sought after leader of conferences and seminars. She has published several books.

Sarah Tucker College for Women

Mission agencies from other denominations have also worked extensively to provide education for women and children in India. The Church Missionary Society, the Society for the Propagation of the Gospel, and the London Missionary Society established major mission institutions for girls. A woman with a disability in far-off England who had never visited India was moved to start schools by the plight of Indian girls prohibited

Of seventy-two members in the Pakistan General Assembly, fourteen are alumnae of Kinnaird College.

Isabella Thoburn College and Kinnaird College are two higher education centers which serve a majority of non-Christian students, and whose faculties are mostly non-Christians. They are models of living in a multifaith environment.

from education. Sarah Tucker, who learned about these girls from her brother, John Taylor, a Secretary for the Church Missionary Society in India, started mission institutions for women in the south of India. A school begun in 1857 that became a college for women in 1885, Sarah Tucker College is one among many stories of witness to education as mission.

Women in Higher Education and the Women's Division

In November 2000, the Women's Division held a Consultation on Women in Higher Education, bringing together presidents and one representative from several of the colleges and universities established by the Woman's Foreign Missionary Society. Nine institutions were represented at the Consultation, including Isabella Thoburn College in India and Kinnaird College in Pakistan. The purpose was to offer a space in which to explore the common heritage and role of each institution, and to share common concerns about women in higher education.

Among these, Isabella Thoburn College and Kinnaird College are two higher education centers which serve a majority of non-Christian students, and whose faculties are mostly non-Christians. They are models of living in a multifaith environment. Intercollegiate exchanges are being facilitated between institutions, including Isabella Thoburn College and Fujian Hwa Nan Women's College in China.

Stuntzabadi village woman examining book from literacy display, Pakistan.

In order to make local and global connections, six historic mission institutions in the United States were also invited to be part of this Women in Higher Education network. Among them are Paine College in Augusta, Georgia, Rust College in Holly Springs, Mississippi, and Clark Atlanta University in Atlanta.[17]

SECONDARY SCHOOLS

Lucy Harrison High School

On a secondary school level, Lucy Harrison Girls' High School in Lahore, the second largest metropolis in Pakistan, was established by the Woman's Foreign Missionary Society of the Methodist Episcopal Church, a predecessor organization of the United Methodist Women. In 1912, Lily Dexter Greene, a Methodist lay missionary, opened a primary school with two rooms. She had a vision of nurturing girls from Christian families and breaking or weakening the caste system prevalent at that time. Most of the Christian converts came from the lower rungs of the caste-based society.

It became a residential school where girls from poor and lower-middle-class families could live and study. Today, there are about one thousand students and among them, one hundred are residential students. The Women's Division continues to support Lucy Harrison Girls' High School, which continues to produce women leaders in Pakistan for church and society. It is "a witness within the Islamic community" as well; a link in "developing interfaith and social harmony within Pakistan, which has become a victim of Islamic religious fundamentalism," according to Bishop Samuel R. Azariah, Bishop of Raiwind, Church of Pakistan.

Under the government of Zulfikar Ali Bhutto, father of former prime minister Benazir Bhutto, the government of Pakistan nationalized the school in 1971. After almost thirty years of being run by the government, the school was returned to church management at the Diocese of Raiwind, Pakistan.

She had a vision of nurturing girls from Christian families and breaking or weakening the caste system prevalent at that time. Most of the Christian converts came from the lower rungs of the caste-based society.

Calcutta Girls' High School

Frances Major, a retired missionary now residing in Brooks-Howell Home, Ashville, N.C., is a former principal of the Calcutta Girls' High School. This school caters to both the elite and the middle class. Major opened the facilities to the underprivileged by starting an evening school there. Recalling her ministry in India, Major said in an interview, "The most significant thing is the change in me.... We have so much to learn from India."[18] Using the metaphor of a journey or pilgrimage ("jatra"), she recounts her life and ministry in her book, *My Indian Jatra: Half a Century Life in India.*

Today many of these institutions are either autonomous institutions or affiliated with universities. Secondary and primary schools are mostly under state governments. They have to compete with their secular counterparts for excellence in education and integrity in administration, keeping their minority Christian witness alive in the midst of other faith majorities.

MEDICAL MISSION

Clara Swain Hospital

Clara Swain was the first female medical missionary doctor sent to India in 1869 by the Women's Foreign Missionary Society of the Methodist Episcopal Church. She started her first medical class in Bareilly, India, with fourteen girls from the Girls' Orphanage and three married students. On seeing a skeleton that

Clara Swain Hospital, Bareilly, India

73

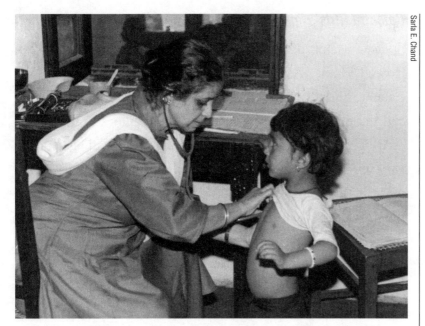

Medical examination being given at Balar Kalui Nilayam School in Chennai (Madras), India.

the doctor had brought from America, a girl in one of her classes exclaimed, "...how will this woman rise in the resurrection with her flesh in America and her bones in India?"[19] The first hospital for women and children in Asia, the hospital continues to provide health care, training for nurses, and community outreach.

The Women's Division has provided a substantial amount of funds to help revitalize Clara Swain Hospital. The General Board of Global Ministries has provided funds to renovate buildings, acquire medical equipment, provide scholarships for staff, and help expand community outreach projects. Today Clara Swain has about one hundred beds. Its community-based projects are thriving.

Vellore Christian College and Hospital

John Scudder was a missionary sent by the American Congregationalists who later transferred to the Reformed Church of America in the 1800s. The story that changed the life and mission of his daughter, Ida Scudder, is legendry in India. On a single night, three pregnant women of different faiths refused to be helped by the male doctor and all three died in childbirth. Because of that tragic occurrence, Ida Scudder, who never wanted to be a missionary, became a medical doctor. In 1903, she opened the Vellore Hospital for Women in India. She also started a training center for women doctors that later admitted men.

Today, the Christian Medical College and Hospital in Vellore is a fifteen-hundred-bed premier teaching institution that is rated among the finest in India. The General Board of Global Ministries of The United Methodist Church has supported it over the years with missionaries and grants for equipment and community health work. The Women's Division helped provide for the new Mother-Child Block completed in 2000, the hospital's centennial year. This medical institution is indeed an ecumenical undertaking.[20]

Today, the Christian Medical College and Hospital in Vellore is a fifteen-hundred-bed premier teaching institution that is rated among the finest in India.

Comprehensive Rural Health Program

On their wedding day in April 1960, two medical doctors in India, Mabelle and Raj Arole, took a vow to work together and devote their lives to the most marginalized and disenfranchised people living in the rural areas. Their innovative contribution, the Comprehensive Rural Health Program in the Indian village of Jamkhed, integrated preventive and curative services. Jamkhed, as the program is known all over the world, is a pioneer in the arena of community-based primary health care.[21] The General Board of Global Ministries has sponsored dozens of community health volunteers from Africa, Asia, and Latin America for training at Jamkhed. The trainees have been instrumental in starting similar models of community health programs in Brazil, Zimbabwe, Sierra Leone, Kenya, and the Philippines. This medical couple has demonstrated that health for all is possible if the professionals in health care and the medical industry are willing to allow such a thing to happen.

JAMKHED, AS THE PROGRAM IS KNOWN ALL OVER THE WORLD, IS A PIONEER IN THE ARENA OF COMMUNITY-BASED PRIMARY HEALTH CARE.

HEALTH AND WELFARE ISSUES IMPACTING WOMEN

HIV/AIDS

Of India's population of over one billion people, almost 1 percent is infected with HIV/AIDS. Though 95 percent of those who live

75

with HIV/AIDS reside in developing countries, only 5 percent of them get the needed medication. The U.S. National Intelligence Council estimates that by the year 2010 there will be twenty to twenty-five million people who are HIV positive in India alone.

The main avenue of the transmission of the virus is heterosexual contact. The absence of the social and political will to address the issue on the part of the government, the unwillingness to talk about this issue from the pulpits, and the stigma attached to the disease have proved detrimental in checking the tide of the rapid spread of the disease.

A hopeful sign is an agreement brought about by the Clinton Foundation. Four pharmaceutical companies are willing to produce anti-retroviral medicines for approximately $140 per patient annually. Some non-governmental organizations have been on the forefront in raising the consciousness of the people and educating them against the spread of the disease.[22]

"Honor Killing"

In a culture where arranged marriage is the norm and a woman is considered mostly as a male's property, if a woman is suspected of an illicit relationship or even perceived to have had one, she is killed by her family in order to preserve its honor. Originally deemed as a remote tribal custom, it occurs regularly in towns and cities of Pakistan. Among the 266 killings reported in Lahore's daily newspapers in 1999, almost 40 percent of the reported killings were under the category of "honor killings."[23]

The Human Rights Commission of Pakistan receives reports of honor killings and advocates on behalf of the victims. Rashid Rahman, a human rights advocate in Multan, Pakistan, says, "People continue to suffer in silence. No one gets justice unless someone powerful intervenes."[24]

The Hadood Ordinances

Introduced by the government of Pakistan to govern the families of Muslims, under these ordinances women are tried for adultery (zina), but men are not. Tragically, rape cases have

The U.S. National Intelligence Council estimates that by the year 2010 there will be twenty to twenty-five million people who are HIV-positive in India alone.

been interpreted as adultery. For the imposition of the maximum penalty under this ordinance, the testimony of women and non-Muslim witnesses is invalid if the accused happens to be a Muslim.[25]

Dowry and Stove Burning

"Mehr" is the dowry given by the groom to the bride under Islamic law. A part of a marriage contract, the original intent was to safeguard a woman in case of widowhood or divorce. In Pakistan, however, low-income women are often denied their dowry. Because of many years of Hindu influence in the Indian subcontinent, there is also the practice of Muslim women giving dowries to their men. This corrupt practice has crept into the Christian church of Pakistan as well as into India. Even though efforts have been made by the governments of both Pakistan and India to curb the dowry practice, or at least to set a limit, in actual practice it has not had much effect. In addition, the horrific practice of killing women by stove-burning is an occurrence in both countries.

Women are adversely affected by the evil of the dowry. Often in Hindu and Christian families there is some form of money or property exchange from the girl's family to the boy's family at the time of marriage. Dowry is a common practice in marriage negotiations. Gold jewelry, twenty to one hundred sovereigns, and modern gadgets such as TV sets, are part of the marriage negotiations. The demand for a higher dowry has resulted in domestic violence after marriage, resulting in ill treatment and even the death of the daughter-in-law. In spite of the Dowry Prohibition Act of 1961 in India and the Amended Acts of 1984 and 1986, the menace of dowry demand has not yet been eliminated. However, several women's groups are working to abolish the dowry system.

The religious sanction of the dowry goes back to Manu, the ancient law giver in 3 BCE. It is among the earliest of the eight marriage rites listed as the "brahma" rite, practiced mostly by Brahmins.[26] The Brahma rite is known as "Kanyadana," or gift

IF A WOMAN IS SUSPECTED OF AN ILLICIT RELATIONSHIP OR EVEN PERCEIVED TO HAVE HAD ONE, SHE IS KILLED BY HER FAMILY IN ORDER TO PRESERVE ITS HONOR.

of the virgin daughter. The father of the bride gives his daughter as a gift to the bridegroom. Along with the gift of his daughter, it is customary for the father to give jewelry and clothing to his daughter.

Contrary to this practice, other castes often practiced "bride-price." The groom gave gifts to the father of the bride in order to obtain her, since her marriage would be a loss to her family. Although this concept is also found in the Old Testament (Jacob worked for Rachel for fourteen years), the selective practice of giving a dowry in the Indian context has a peculiar class base.

The Report of the National Committee on the Status of Women diagnoses the reason for the shift from bride-price to dowry. Their analysis is that since the dowry is associated with higher social groups, it is an attempt to improve the social status of a family or group.[27] In some Christian circles in India, especially in the South, the more educated a woman is, the more dowry she has to give.

Due to the conflict and incessant demands over dowry even after marriage, there have been attempted murders of women by stove-burning. In this horrific practice, gas that is used as fuel for stoves is poured over the woman, and then the woman is set on fire. The perpetrators are usually the in-laws or husbands of these victims. The police often record these cases as accidents that occurred in the kitchen while the woman was cooking.

The majority of instances of domestic violence within families

Due to the conflict and incessant demands over dowry even after marriage, there have been attempted murders of women by stove-burning. In this horrific practice, gas that is used as fuel for stoves is poured over the woman, and then the woman is set on fire.

Toge Fujihira

Biology class at Kinnaird College for Women, Lahore, Pakistan

Woman standing beside soup tureen at Reay Road-Tamil Project Daycare in Mumbai (Bombay), India. This one room serves as a daycare, kitchen, and Bible study.

In the public perception, a girl child in India does not have the status and value of a male child. In the last fifteen years, genetic testing to determine the sex of the child has been an increasing medical practice.

are due to the heavy demand for a dowry by the husband and his family. Unfortunately, such cases are not fully documented, though women's groups are now organizing themselves to protect women.

Female Infanticide and Foeticide

In the Bible there are unflinching accounts of the killings of male children by the Pharaoh and King Herod. In India, female foeticide, the killing of the female fetus, is a sad reality, often chosen willingly by pregnant mothers. Many times, it goes unrecorded.

In the public perception, a girl child in India does not have the status and value of a male child. In the last fifteen years, genetic testing to determine the sex of the child has been an increasing medical practice. In China, South Korea, and India, this test has become more popular than anywhere else in the world. Female foeticide has been reported in many states in India. As a result, the overall ratio of women to men in India is very unbalanced. In India, 18 percent more girls than boys die before their fifth birthday. The strong preference for a son is a sad reality in India.

According to a UNICEF report of 1999, female foeticide has been reported in twenty-seven of the thirty-two states in India.

In some places, the states of Bihar and Rajastan, for example, the birth ratio of girls to boys is significantly lower than the norm—sixty females to one hundred males.[28]

With the infant mortality rate of India indicating more girls than boys dying before their fifth birthdays, records are beginning to be kept. Though infectious diseases attack both male and female children in the same way and though female children have the "female biological edge" with more "robust" health at birth, female children are often the victims of certifiable neglect.[29] In 1984, there were forty thousand known cases of foeticide, and 84 percent of gynecologists in Bombay admitted to performing sex-determination medical tests.[30] Unfortunately, tradition and modern technology could work against female children. This extreme interpretation and practice of pro-choice, based on the internalization of patriarchy, could have tragic results for the subcontinent.

Women's Invisible Work

A woman's work is often invisible in Pakistan and India. From dawn to dusk, many women work inside their homes caring, nurturing, looking after their children, and cooking food for their families. This household work as well as all the agricultural work women do is invisible. Only women who go out to work and bring money home are counted as "gainfully" employed. Some

"The foremost issue is untouchability on the basis of caste. The second, poverty. The third important issue is religious fundamentalism."

—Bishop Jeyapaul David, President, National Council of Churches in India at the National Council of Churches quadrennial Assembly held in Sarah Tucker College, Tirunelveli, Chennai, India, February 10-13, 2004.

Sarla E. Chand

Community Rural Health Program office in Jamkhed, India

women spend many hours a day fetching firewood and water. In Pakistan, especially in the North West Frontier near the border with Afghanistan, women have to walk miles to fetch water. Women in both India and Pakistan carry heavy loads of water on their heads or hips, even during pregnancies. On average, unpaid work done by women is anywhere from six to ten hours a day.

MISSION AND THE LINGERING REMNANTS OF COLONIALISM

Post-colonial writers have looked at the mission endeavors of education, health care, and other ministries and exposed remnants of colonialism and cultural imperialism. While there are records and images of missionaries seeking to serve "heathens," thereby revealing paternalism and colonialism, there are also the affectionate narratives of students and the beneficiaries of these schools and colleges. In the fields of education and health, missionary institutions have paved the way for improving and developing lives. Many Hindu and Muslim girls are the beneficiaries of education in Christian schools.[31] Some "secret Christians" have emerged out of some of these schools—girls and young women from the institutions who were afraid of becoming Christians openly, but who nevertheless professed Christ. This is a phenomenon that still goes unrecorded, for obvious reasons, on school campuses.

Christian mission to women and girls in the subcontinent is a major contribution, despite its shortcomings. Steering clear of colonialist undertones, Christian witness now has to confront fundamentalist trends of the majority religions without succumbing to a fundamentalism of its own brand of Christianity.

DALITS: THE "UNTOUCHABLES"

The *Rig Veda*, an ancient Hindu religious text written around 1000 BCE, outlines the vision of a caste-based society. Caste itself is envisioned as God's body parts.

The Brahmin was his mouth.
The arms were made the prince,
His thighs the common people,
And from his feet the serf was born.[32]

The first four, as delineated previously, are the Brahmins, Kshatriyas, Vaisyas, and Shudras. The so-called untouchables are not even included in the imagined body parts of God. They are a fifth category of people called Panchamas.

For Dalit Christians, therefore, the Christian notion of the Body of Christ is a difficult reality to live in, for culture and religion have excluded these Christians from God's body for so long. Even Christian religious practices have not been an exception. Dalit theologians struggle within this context to proclaim the liberation of the gospel.

There are two hundred fifty million Dalits in India, the so-called black untouchables. One out of every six Indians bears the impact of discrimination.[33] Dalits are the aboriginals of India, oppressed by the weight of caste for the last three thousand years. Gandhi, a non-Dalit, tried to integrate Dalits within Hinduism. He called them "Harijans," people of God. For the Dalits, however, the name evoked pity and sympathy. They preferred the name Dalits, meaning "broken" people.

Gandhi toured India where Dalits were excluded from temples, village wells, restaurants and washing places. He challenged customs that barred them from full integration into society. However, the deeply-wounded Dalits, weighed down by centuries of oppression, felt that Gandhi "romanticized Indian cultural heritage and advocated the integration of Dalits within Hinduism." For them, such an attempt has "totally failed."[34] This is often the voice of the educated Dalits. Their wounded cry is that Gandhi underestimated the vicious power of casteism within Hinduism, and thus he failed to reject Hinduism. Gandhi's failure is the failure of those of us who speak *for* the oppressed and not *as one of them*. Dalits turned to Dr. B. R. Ambedkar, a Dalit himself.

A word picture might illuminate the plight of Dalits in India. It is a metaphor minted at the kiln of the rural consciousness of India and in the crucible of agony in the soul of the leader of the "untouchables," Dr. B. R. Ambedkar. The "Father of the Indian Constitution," Ambedkar is himself a Dalit.

The Hindu caste system is like a pyramid of earthenware pots set one on top of the other. The Brahmins and Kshatriyas are at the top, while the Shudras and the untouchables are at the bottom. Within each earthenware pot, men are placed at the top and women of that caste are placed at the bottom like "crushed and wasted powder." Ambedkar pinpoints the vicious clutches of the caste system when he says, "At the very bottom of the Dalits and below them are the suppressed Dalit women."[35] A Dalit woman, stacked at the bottom of the earthenware pots, is "broken" and "crushed" by multiple layers of oppression. Let us take off our shoes lest we trample on the broken spirits of the pyramid.

Bishop James Mathews, a former executive secretary of the Division of World Missions with the Board of Missions of The Methodist Church, records a momentous story in his book, *South of the Himalayas*, about Dr. Ambedkar's decision to leave Hinduism. It is a painful story etched in the ethical consciousness of the Indians. A visitor called on Ambedkar in 1946, a year before the independence of India. On his mantelpiece was a picture of the Buddha. There was also a picture of Jesus before Pilate. The visitor asked Ambedkar whether he was not deciding what to do with Jesus. Ambedkar said that his guess was right.

It was a time when Ambedkar was wondering, as a Dalit in the new India, which religion would be befitting for him. In a couple of years, Ambedkar made the decision to choose Buddhism,[36] a religion which originated as a revolt against Hindu Brahminical practices. His choice encouraged Dalits in great numbers to embrace Buddhism.

Referring to this incident, Tremayne Copplestone, writing for the General Board of Global Ministries of The United Methodist Church in 1973, aptly says,

The advent into Christianity of masses of Harijans under Ambedkar's leadership was—if it ever actually constituted a real opportunity for the Church—a lost opportunity as far as Methodism was concerned.[37]

Sadly, this is true. The Body of Christ in India has been suffering from the evil of casteism, too. At an interview with the Convener of the National Federation of Dalit Women in India, Ruth Manorama, a Christian, asked a group of ecumenical women leaders, "Can the church say, 'we do not have gold or silver, but the power of Christ'?"[38] A similar tide of events has been happening in the West. African American and Hispanic youth have been leaving the fold of Christianity for Islam. Discrimination within church and society has often driven them in great numbers away from their original spiritual home, Christianity.

In the World Conference Against Racism in Durban, South Africa, in 2001, Dalits raised the consciousness of many participants from all over the world about "apartheid" in India. The U.S. Congressional Bill 4215 on Human Rights in India brought to light, for the first time, U.S. Congressional recognition of the Dalit plight in India. However, the U.S. walked out of this world conference in South Africa.

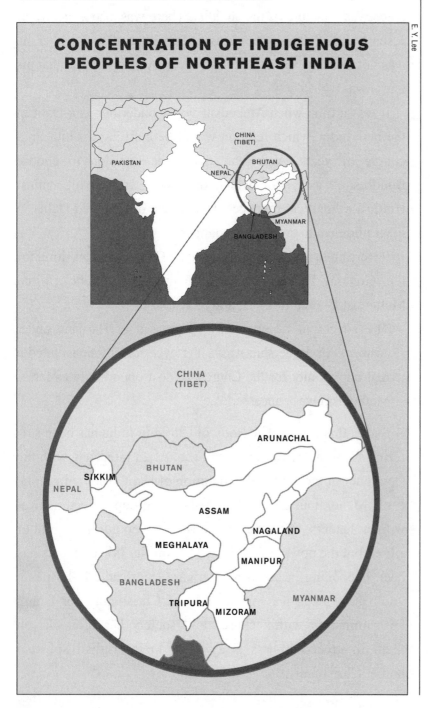

CONCENTRATION OF INDIGENOUS PEOPLES OF NORTHEAST INDIA

E. Y. Lee

Rape, often used as a weapon of war, is used against the Dalit woman by upper caste employers in rural and agricultural India, where her husband is often a "bonded laborer," sold to slavery.

My name is Anusuya. I am a Dalit woman, wife of a bonded laborer. My husband sought liberation from his former employer and my state government also gave my husband freedom. Along with freedom, we were also given an acre of land to rehabilitate us. Alas, my husband's landlord took that land immediately. Therefore my husband went to the local government's head office to get our land back.

My husband's former "owner" was enraged at the freedom of my husband and his courage at seeking local recourse. The owner decided to teach my husband a lesson. I was the object of that cruel lesson. I was gang-raped on a banana plantation in a village near Shimoga in the state of Karnataka. My story is the story of countless Dalit women across the subcontinent.[39]

Pots within pots, crushed from above and sideways. In their earthenwares, often in broken shards, Dalit women carry on the stories of survival, resilience, and sheer courage in the face of violence in its stark nakedness.

A group of people listed by the Indian government as Scheduled Tribes are indigenous peoples, physically isolated from the rest of the society, who live in mountainous and hilly areas separated from the main states of India by Nepal and Bangladesh (see map). A particular area where indigenous peoples are more concentrated is Northeast India. It is an area of diversity, with many languages and ethnicities, most of them belonging to the Mongoloid race. The indigenous people of Mongol origin are called "tribal," not by their own choice, but by the designation of the Indian government. "It is not a redeeming status," according to an indigenous female theologian, Professor Lalrinawmi Ralte, since it connotes negative associations of being primitive, inferior, and savage.[40]

Human Rights

A key issue among the Northeast Indian indigenous peoples is the violation of their human rights. There have been insurgency movements; some demanding self-determination, others seeking a separate state for indigenous people within India. The imposition of the Armed Forces Act of 1958, with special powers for army officers, has been harmful to the lives of the indigenous communities. The Act gave power to officers in the armed forces to shoot and kill. The contention of many indigenous peoples, including indigenous theologians, is that sectarian violence in mainland India (see map) is not met with such severity.[41]

Human Rights has been picked up as a key issue by indigenous theologians. In an interview Professor Lalrinawmi Ralte referred to the "boundary mistakes" committed by the British as well as the Central Government of India (the Federal Government) in dividing the peoples into states.[42] These artificial boundaries divided the same ethnic group into different states.

Christianity and Indigenous Peoples

Many denominations have worked among the indigenous peoples. The Roman Catholics, the Presbyterians (including the

Welsh Presbyterian Mission), the American Baptists, and the Australia and New Zealand Baptists have had the most significant presence. Mission agencies from the West worked on what is known as a "comity arrangement" in their work in India (see Chapter 5 for more about its relation to the role of Methodist mission).

There has been a rapid growth in Christianity in this region. The total Christian population of northeast India is about 4.3 million and it comprises 22.7 percent of Indian Christians. Mizoram, a state in northeast India, is 85 percent Christian, of which a particular indigenous group, called Mizo people, comprise 99 percent. Among the five hundred women theologians in Northeast India, only a handful have been ordained—one by the Ao Baptist Church in the state of Nagaland; another by the Manipur Baptist Church in the state of Manipur.[43]

An ongoing dilemma is to combine indigenous practices and Christianity. The westernized form of Christianity has rooted itself both among the indigenous and in mainland Christianity. Especially among the indigenous peoples, the ecological crisis has brought to light the need for their ancient respect for nature to be mainstreamed, an insight that mainland Christians have yet to incorporate.

A Handful of Rice

In the Northeast and many places in the South of the subcontinent, Christian women had the practice of putting aside a handful of rice for the furtherance of the gospel before they cooked their meals. Lalrinawami Ralte mentions that the Mizoram Presbyterian Church, which appointed Bible Women as far back as 1913, did not have funding to support these women who would go to places where the missionaries would not be able to go. In the Northeast, the work of the Bible Women among the Mizo indigenous group was supported only by "the handful of rice project by women."[44] Women in other parts of the country also set aside a handful of rice for the mission work of women. Often, the work of the Bible Women, the catechists who have

The total Christian population of northeast India is about 4.3 million and comprises 22.7 percent of Indian Christians. Mizoram, a state in northeast India, is 85 percent Christian, of which a particular indigenous group, called Mizo people, comprise 99 percent.

been supportive workers with the missionaries, and later on, the pastors, goes under-reported.

Fellowship of the Least Coin

The concept of the Fellowship of the Least Coin came about as a vision from Shanti Solomon of India. In 1956, she was part of a team of seven women sponsored by the Presbyterian Church (U.S.A.) that visited several Asian countries after World War II to work for peace and development. Denied a visa to enter Korea, she had to wait in the Philippines. While waiting in disappointment and frustration, she reflected on the economic and political fences that arise as women travel, that separate them from one another.

After the team returned, she suggested the idea of Christian prayer and an action to accompany it: a "least coin" set aside for God's work. Now the Fellowship of the Least Coin is a global ecumenical movement of prayer for peace, healing, and mending relationships across the international fences.

The Chipko Movement

In 1973, some women in a village in India joined together to protect their forests and trees when commercial timbermen came to cut them. The women formed a circle around the trees and were successful in their resistance. Chipko literally means "embrace" or "hug." These "tree huggers" protected thousands of trees in the Himalayan forest. The Chipko Movement, as it came to be called, spread all over the foothills of the Himalayas. The humble yet daring effort of a group of ordinary women gave birth to a movement to save the ecology of the largest mountain range in the world.

Child Labor

In 1995, a twelve-year-old youth in Canada started an organization called Kids Can Free the Children. While searching for the comics in a local paper, Craig Keilburger read about Iqbal Masih, a young boy in Pakistan. Sold at the age of four into slavery, Masih worked as a child laborer in the carpet-weaving industry. After six years of child labor, Masih began to organize

The average American's energy use is equivalent to the consumption of thirty-two Indians.

children in the carpet industry, and at the age of twelve, he was killed for speaking out against child labor in the country. On reading this, Kielburger began his advocacy work on behalf of victims of child labor.

In 1996, Human Rights Watch published *The Small Hands of Slavery: Bonded Child Labor in India*.[45] It documented the extensive use of child labor in industries such as silver, synthetic gemstones, silk, leather, agriculture, and carpet weaving. About 115 million children are working as laborers in India. In 1997, the Supreme Court of India ordered India's National Human Rights Commission to supervise laws enacted to punish employers of children in hazardous labor. United Methodist Women has been engaged in the Rugmark Campaign to eradicate child labor in the subcontinent.

Refugees

The influx of refugees into Pakistan from Afghanistan adds to the already existing problems in Pakistan. Refugees flee from Afghanistan due to drought, violence, and war. Church World Service (CWS), supported by the United Methodist Church, funds support work among the refugees and teaches them skills. Working with local non-government organizations, Church World Service has begun quilting projects. Women earn 50 rupees (85 cents) by making a quilt a day. The quilts are distributed to displaced people within Afghanistan as well as to refugees in Pakistan. Afghanistan women refugees, in groups of eight to ten, share stories of pain and joy and piece together lives of hope and rehabilitation as well as quilts for themselves and others.[46]

India's lifestyle is very different from the lifestyle in the United States. While the Global South is impacting the fragility of the earth negatively by growing population, the Global North must take responsibility for the impact of growing consumption patterns.[47] Although we in the United States comprise 5 percent of the total population of the world, we use 25 percent of the world's resources. We generate more trash than many

MASIH BEGAN TO ORGANIZE CHILDREN IN THE CARPET INDUSTRY AND AT THE AGE OF TWELVE, HE WAS KILLED FOR SPEAKING OUT AGAINST CHILD LABOR IN THE COUNTRY.

countries of the world combined. The average American's energy use is equivalent to the consumption of thirty-two Indians. The lifestyles and consumption patterns of the United States are depleting planet earth's resources at a rapid rate. About 2.5 million Americans have the environmental impact of nearly eighty million people of India.

Dorothy Sampathkumar, President of the Women's Society of Christian Service (WSCS), in India, says that she has been much impressed by the missional commitment of United Methodist women in the United States. Since they began their work 135 years ago with two cents and a prayer, she says,

women missionaries left a lasting impact on the work and lives they touched. Through their stewardship of personal service, they placed Jesus the Light in many a home and life. The light that was passed on to us still shines on as we, the Indian people of God, strive to keep bearing witness to this Light. Pray with us as we pray for you that the light of the gospel will bring hope to the lost and needy.[48]

A_bout 2.5 million Americans have the environmental impact of nearly eighty million people of India.

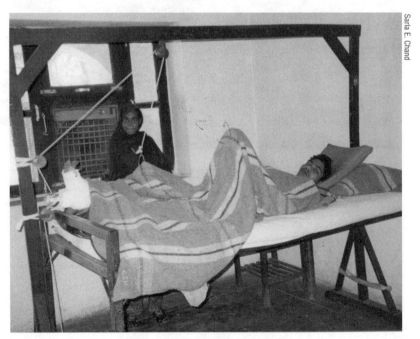

Patient at Clara Swain Hospital in Bareilly, India

Sarla E. Chand

Methodist Church in Bangalore, India

5

THEOLOGIES AND MISSIOLOGIES FROM INDIA

BY JACOB S. DHARMARAJ, PH.D.

WHETHER IN EAST OR WEST, THE SENSE OF RELEASE AND FREEDOM IN GETTING YOURSELF OFF YOUR OWN HANDS AND INTO THE HANDS OF GOD IS THE SAME....WHEN YOU ARE IN THE HANDS OF GOD, YOU ARE WHERE YOU BELONG. THIS IS HOME.

—E. STANLEY JONES IN HIS BOOK, *CONVERSION*

Indian and Pakistani Christians live in religiously pluralistic and culturally diverse situations. They have to define their theological beliefs and exercise their missional principles in unambiguous ways in order to suit the context in which they live. In this process, they theologize their mission principles and missionize their Christian beliefs in order to remain faithful to their calling as a Christian community.

HISTORIC ORIGIN

Historically, theology in India can be traced back to the earliest period of St. Thomas Christians who were living in the southwestern part of India. Their theology was derived not from written materials, but from their traditional hymns, prayers, and the liturgy they practiced and observed. Their primary concern was not to develop a written theology but to exercise their faith and to observe religious practices that reflected on the new life they received from God in Christ.

However, the formation of contemporary Indian Christian theology could be traced to the development that took place in the late eighteenth and nineteenth centuries under the watchful eyes of colonizers. After political independence in 1947, Indian Christians strived to develop a theology that would fit the particular Indian context. In their struggle to create an Indian Christian theology, Indian Christians focused on an action-oriented theology, a theology of mission, free of Western influence.

Unlike traditional Western theology, which is based on metaphysical speculations, Indian theology is formed in the context of the living reality of diverse religions, various cultures, a mixture of races and a commingling of classes of people who speak many languages, the poverty of the masses, and national identity. Indian theology is formed, sustained, and determined by the mission and ministry of the church in India through its affirmation that the God who is revealed in Jesus Christ is on the side of the poor, the marginalized, and the oppressed. Hence, Indian theology is a contextual theology. It is from below. It is participatory in its method and function.

When one thinks of Indian Christianity, notable Christian leaders come to mind, such as the Apostle Thomas, Francis Xavier, Robert De Nobili, Alexander Duff, William Carey, C. F. Andrews, E. Stanley Jones, Krishna Mohan Bannerji, Pandita Ramabai, Narayan Vamam Tilak, M. M. Thomas, and Mother Teresa.

Although these Christian leaders have contributed so much to the cause of the church and people in India, countless others have also worked hard under difficult circumstances in order to make the Church of Jesus Christ a living witness. The following is a broad outline of their contributions toward the development of the Indian Christian theology.

Influence of Hindu Thought

The early Indian Christian theology was developed not by Christians but by Hindu reformers who sought to reform the Indian society and revitalize Hindu religions. Consequently, they imitated Christian values and Christ's teachings. Although Hindu

Unlike traditional Western theology, which is based on metaphysical speculations, Indian theology is formed in the context of the living reality of diverse religions, various cultures, a mixture of races and a commingling of classes of people who speak many languages, the poverty of the masses, and national identity.

Dr. Cherian Thomas, shown with then Bishop, Victor Raja, and Dr. Singh opening the newly-renovated—and GBGM-funded—emergency room and lab area of the Clara Swain Hospital, in 2002.

orthodoxy and Indian religions are tradition-bound and difficult to reconcile with Christianity, those reformers worked hand-in-glove with the early missionaries to transform Indian society.

These Hindu reformers did not address some of the key concepts in Hinduism. For instance, the Hindu interpretation of sin and salvation is more individualistic. Its concept of rebirth and eternity sustains the caste system and untouchability. Its acceptance of "karma" (fate) and "dharma" (right conduct) fosters belief in service and passive acceptance of one's lot in life. The reformers embraced Christian teachings and values without fully comprehending its prophetic and advocacy roles.

Raja Ram Mohan Roy (1772-1833), a Hindu Brahmin from Bengal, was influenced by Jesus' teachings on the love of neighbor. He started a reform movement and wrote *The Precepts of Jesus, the Guide to Peace and Happiness* in 1820. He established Brahmo Samaj, a Hindu reform society, in 1828 and initiated a dialogue between Christianity and Hinduism. He supported the missionaries in the abolition of widow-burning, child-marriage, and other social evils. However, he rejected the divinity of Jesus and worked primarily for the self-assertions of the Hindu faith in response to the European understanding of Indian religious traditions. Kaj Baago says, "The first persons

Mohandas Gandhi in New Delhi, India in 1947

They taught that all human beings are made in the image and likeness of God, and that "karma" cannot determine the fate of the human lot, especially their class and caste in society.

to attempt an indigenous interpretation of Christ in India were neither missionaries nor Indian Christians, but Brahmo Samajists," members of the Hindu reform society.[1]

Keshub Chandra Sen (1833-1884), another Hindu reformer, underscored Jesus' racial identity as an Asian and compared the Christian doctrine of the Trinity with Sat (being), Cit (consciousness) and Ananda (bliss). He called for Hindu converts to reject European influence and to develop Indian religious theology. Bankin Chandra Chatterjee (1838-1894), Jyotiba Phule (1827-1890), Bal Gangadhar Tilak (1856-1920), Vivekananda (1863-1902), Babasaheb Ambedkar (1891-1956), Mahatma Gandhi (1869-1948), and Sarvepalli Radhakrishnan (1888-1975) are some of the Indian leaders who worked to reform Hindu Indian society, while supporting peace, justice, and equality.

These leaders went against the grain of a society deeply entrenched in the caste system and the belief in reincarnation, which justified the exploitation of the poor and the underclass. They taught that all human beings are made in the image and likeness of God, and that "karma" cannot determine the fate of the human lot, especially their class and caste in society.

Twentieth-century Hindu philosophers and leaders such as Aurobindo Ghose, Sarvepalli Radhakrishnan, and Mahatma Gandhi studied the gospels and were influenced by the teachings of the Bible. For instance, Mahatma Gandhi's use of the principle of non-violence and the struggle against untouchability drew on the Sermon on the Mount. In the larger context, even the constitution of India was modeled after Western Christian humanism.

"Evangelize the World. . ."

The turn of the twentieth century was the height of colonialism and missionary expansion. The Indian subcontinent was contained and unified under British colonial rule. Law and order prevailed as had not been the case in previous centuries. The European trade monopoly was firmly established and travel became easy and safe.

The scars of the 1857 Sepoy Mutiny were healed and nationalistic movements were silenced. Inter-European rivalry was quelled. The increasing influence of the orientalists' publications, missionaries' reports, travel literature, commercial enterprise, and colonial government enabled more and more young missionaries to go to India. A focused and specialized form of evangelization was designed to evangelize India.

Following in the footsteps of women such as Isabella Thoburn and Clara Swain, single female missionaries began to travel to India. Mission societies began to gain more converts through group conversions, known as "mass movements," among those classes that suffered most from the existing social, cultural, and economic order.[2]

FOLLOWING IN THE FOOTSTEPS OF WOMEN SUCH AS ISABELLA THOBURN AND CLARA SWAIN, SINGLE FEMALE MISSIONARIES BEGAN TO TRAVEL TO INDIA.

Edinburgh Conference

The World Missionary Conference held in Edinburgh, Scotland in 1910 was attended by over twelve hundred missionaries, most of them serving in India and Africa. Seventeen Asians attended the conference as delegates of British and American mission societies. South American and Roman Catholic representatives were not included in the conference. Neither political liberation nor human and social development issues were included in the agenda.

Conference leaders made the assertion that Christianity is the fulfillment of all religions. They supported the theory that non-Christian religions and Eastern cultures do not have elements for salvation, and that Christianity in its Western form is the only path to salvation.

One of the participants who attended the International Missionary Council in Edinburgh was V. S. Azariah, a native of India. A product of the Church Missionary Society, an Anglican mission organization in India, Azariah envisioned an Indian church with Indian leadership. When he saw only a handful of non-European delegates present at a conference whose purpose was actually to evangelize the non-European countries, Azariah challenged the Western paternalistic attitude and called for partnership in mission.

He addressed the predominantly Western delegates to the conference saying, "You have given your goods to feed the poor. You have given your bodies to be burned. We also ask for love. Give us friends."[3] It was a cry for the practice of mutuality in mission.

Soon after the Edinburgh Conference, changes in international politics, the onset of World War I, the emergence of the U.S. as a power, and the rise of Indian nationalistic movements began to affect the mission work in India. Upon their return from Edinburgh, V. S. Azariah and G. S. Eddy, two Indian delegates to the conference, called for a meeting in Chennai in 1912. They encouraged participants to develop an eclectic

"You have given your goods to feed the poor. You have given your bodies to be burned. We also ask for love. Give us friends."

Azariah's striking contribution to the indigenization of Christianity is the Dornakal Cathedral Church of the Ephiphany (situated in South India). It synthesized several architectural styles, combining the domes of Muslim mosques with the pillars of South Indian Hindu temples. The symbols incorporated in the cathedral are a synthesis as well: twelve pillars bearing the church nave for the twelve apostles, lotus flowers to represent India, a datura flower for death, and an offshoot of a banana tree for life. All these are placed under the cross, the symbol of the ultimate reconciliation with God in Christ. The entire cathedral was hand-carved and built by local people over a period of twenty-five years.

mission theology without Western confessional teaching. K. T. Paul, V. S. Azariah, V. Santiago, and others pushed aside the call for the evangelization of India in this generation and planned to indigenize all the mission and outreach organizations on Indian soil. Under their leadership, the National Missionary Society was formed. In 1919, they met in Tranquebar under the leadership of V. S. Azariah, who was the first national bishop of the Anglican church in India.

Azariah and the representatives of the South Indian United Church accepted a resolution for the union of the two major Indian denominations and crafted a document that came to be known as the "Tranquebar Manifesto." It declares:

> We believe that the challenges of the present hour in the period of the reconstruction after the war in the gathering together of the nations, and the present critical situation in India itself, call us to mourn our past divisions and turn to our Lord Jesus Christ to seek in Him the unity of the body expressed in one visible Church. We face together the titanic task of the winning of India for Christ one-fifth of the human race. Yet, confronted by such an overwhelming responsibility, we find ourselves rendered weak and relatively impotent by our unhappy divisions, divisions for which we were not responsible, and which have been, as it were imposed upon us from without; division which we did not create, and which we do not perpetuate.[4]

This union paved the way for the formation of the Church of South India in 1947, one of the earliest and the largest union of Christian denominations in church history.

One of the pioneers in indigenizing the Christian theology and employing Indian symbols was a young Christian named A. J. Appasamy (who later became a bishop of the Church of South India). He proposed a new theology free of Western thought. He compared the mystic elements (*Logos*) found in John's Gospel with the Bhakti Marga (Devotional Path) in Hinduism. Later, he was joined by new Hindu converts like

P. Chenchiah and his brother V. Chakkarai Chetty, both lawyers. They formed a Christian book club and the Christian Samaj, a counter organization to Brahmo Samaj, was established.

Appasamy and other Indian theologians argued that if Christianity as practiced by the Europeans had comfortably incorporated Hebrew tradition, Greek philosophy, and continental existentialism, Indian Christianity could also borrow from its local, cultural, and philosophical tradition to enrich Christianity and make it relevant to the Indian Christian's cultural milieu.

Interfaith and Mission

The International Missionary Council organized another conference in Jerusalem in 1928 to discuss the theology of mission to people of other faiths. The conference was overshadowed by the debate between William Hocking, an American philosopher teaching at Harvard University, and Hendrick Kraemer, a Dutch missionary working in Indonesia. Hocking argued that since Christianity and other religions have so much in common, followers of other religions need not be converted. Kraemer countered that other religions do not have the gift of Jesus Christ, especially the Christian concept of the forgiveness of sins. No consensus was achieved during the conference.

The next major conference was held in Tambaram, Chennai, India in 1938. It was dominated by conservative theologians and missionaries from the West. Here Hendrick Kraemer asserted that in other religions all truth is relative and that the final truth revealed in the person of Jesus Christ is unattainable to them. He and others insisted that there must be a radical discontinuity of Christianity from other religions. The conference was dominated by this debate and as a result the Indian Christian identity, the future of the church in India, and the struggles of the Indian people were not taken seriously. The conference came to an abrupt end as World War II broke out.

Hocking argued that since Christianity and other religions have so much in common, followers of other religions need not be converted.

Kraemer countered that other religions do not have the gift of Jesus Christ, especially the Christian concept of the forgiveness of sins. No consensus was achieved during the conference.

Bishop James Mathews, son-in-law of E. Stanley Jones, said in an interview that Jones "recovered effective evangelism" in the exposition of the concept of the kingdom of God, in the context of Christian faith, and with the relevance of Christianity in India.[5]

Thoroughly at home in India, Jones knew that the kingdom of God is the core principle to live by in a country with a plurality of religions, cultures, and languages. Jones was adept at drawing from the deep springs of Jesus' notions of the kingdom of God, adapting them to the Indian context, and endearing the Christ to the multireligious people of India. Kingdom as well as "kin-dom" of God is still a key to unlocking the doors to interfaith understandings in today's America.

Another book by Jones, *Gandhi: Portrayal of a Friend*, is an affectionate and scholarly tribute to Mahatma Gandhi. A passage in this book was instrumental in shaping the missional direction of Martin Luther King Jr. in using nonviolence as a key strategy in the Civil Rights Movement. Matthews recalled this passage from Jones' book in the context of a conversation he had with King:

> Nonviolence was accepted out of necessity. And yet out of choice. And further: Undoubtedly an overruling Providence was using India as a proving ground for a new type of power—the power of the soul. But the Mahatma repudiated with all his might the idea that the method of truth and non-violence was used because you are weak and cowardly. He insisted that it was the method of the strong, and only the method of the strong. [6]

These were the words that clinched King's decision to launch the Civil Rights Movement on the founding principle of nonviolence. For Eunice Matthews and James Matthews, daughter and son-in-law of Jones, historical influences such as these are a witness to the contagious spirit of the power of nonviolence.

E. Stanley Jones and the Ashram Movement

One of the few missionaries to India who combined evangelical fervor with the political aspirations of the natives of the country was E. Stanley Jones. He was a close friend of Mahatma Gandhi and encouraged Indian Christians to follow Christ without compromising their identity as Indian citizens. He stood in the Wesleyan theological tradition of spiritual transformation that leads to social transformation.

A missionary under the Board of Missions of the Methodist Episcopal Church, Jones wrote *The Christ of the Indian Road*, which revolutionized missional thinking. Capturing Indian mysticism and asceticism in a Christian mode, Jones pioneered the Christian Ashram Movement in the West. An ashram is a place of spiritual retreat, often a forest retreat, used by Hindus for enrichment. Jones also helped establish the Indian ashram within Christian disciplines as a means of drawing men and women together for days at a time to seek through their own quest, to study in depth, and to dialogue. Sat Tal Ashram, founded by Jones in the foothills of the Himalayas, is still a center for spiritual renewal. Currently there are thirty ashrams in the United States.

A cell of the kingdom of God, the ashram draws people from different nationalities, races, religions, classes, and professions in order to learn and study as one family[7]—a "kin-dom" indeed.[8] In India, many came to these ashrams to refute the Christian gospel. Many others came to accept the gospel and Jesus as a way of life.

Chapter 2 includes the story of James Lawson, who worked with Martin Luther King Jr. It details Lawson's trip to India to learn non-violence as a method and strategy from Gandhi. Gandhi and Jones comprise a beautiful chapter in the history of India and Indian Christianity, cherished affectionately in the hearts of millions of Indians. Gandhi is called the Mahatma (Great Soul), and Jones is referred to as the "Missionary Extraordinary" by the *World Outlook* magazine.

Ashram: a place of spiritual retreat, often a forest retreat, used by Hindus for enrichment.

Theological Development After Independence

One event pivotal to the development of Indian Christian theology was the formation of the Church of South India. Fourteen major denominations in south India joined together to form the union (American Methodists, Lutherans, Syrian Orthodox, Marthoma, and a few Baptist churches did not join). When news of the union was announced across the globe, the entire ecclesiastical world rejoiced.

In the global Christian arena the years between 1946 and 1961 were a period of consolidation, cooperation, and a call for oneness and unity between the International Missionary Council and the World Council of Churches that had been established in 1948. On Sunday, November 19, 1961, at the Third Assembly of the World Council of Churches held in New Delhi, two organizations were united into one single entity, which would henceforth bear the name World Council of Churches.

In North India, the Church of North India was established in 1970. All the major denominations except the Lutherans, American Methodists, and Baptists joined together to form the union. The independent and Pentecostal churches have never been part of the negotiations and have not joined the union (one reason the American Methodists did not join was in order to continue to have denominational ties with the United States and to retain their property rights in India). These large church unions in India paved the way not only for the development of ecumenical theology in India, but for the creation of theologies from many ethnic and sub-ethnic communities.

THEOLOGIES OF THE SUBCONTINENT TODAY

The theology of mission in India has changed considerably since the early 1960s, particularly after the Vatican II Conference held in 1962 under the guidance of Pope John XXIII, and the World Council of Churches conference held in New Delhi in 1961.

Historically, the Catholic position is that there is no salvation outside the Roman Catholic Church. People were incorporated into the Church through baptism, the only means of salvation. Such a view was termed the church-centered (ecclesiocentric) theology of mission. After Vatican II, the Pope declared that the Church must update itself, reach beyond its visible boundaries, and open the doors and windows to let a fresh wind blow through the Vatican. The Council recognized that non-Christians who genuinely seek the unknown God are related in various ways to the people of God. Most of the mainline Protestant churches in India believed and practiced a Bible-centered (bibliocentric) theology and Christ-centered (Christocentric) mission practices brought by Western missionaries. The Bible-centered and Christ-centered mission theologies emphasized Christ as the only way to salvation and stressed the importance of Baptism, Holy Communion, and the fellowship of the church. Such beliefs and practices set the Protestant Christian denominations in India on a collision course with the followers of other religions. Hence, Indian theologians such as M. M. Thomas, Raymundo Panikkar, Gavin D'Costa, Stanley J. Samartha, and a few others not only refused the traditional view that all other religions are invalid, but they also called for committed openness "to the point where conversion cannot be precluded—hopefully on both sides."[9]

These theologians also argued that traditional concepts of theology brought by Western mission societies failed to meet concrete realities such as oppression, exploitation, and dehumanization, especially the powerlessness and marginalization of the Dalits and the poor. They argued that varieties of theological expression based on local mission developments needed to be developed, theologies that would correspond to the diverse and varied historical and social fabric of the subcontinent.

Some Indian theologians advocated that Christ is already present in other religions, though hidden and unacknowledged. According to this position, God is impartial, compassionate, and speaks equally through other religions. Hence, the sacred

Dr. Evangeline Anderson Rajkumar, Dean of United Theological College, Bangalore, India, offers a challenge to mainline theologians. The Dalit issue is not just another perspective, she says, but a priority issue. Dalit theology cannot be done by one's head; it is more of a "somatic" theology. Rajkumar emphasizes that Dalit theology opens the face of God; it uncovers the face of God among people. There should not be Indian Christian theology and Dalit theology. They should become part of each other.

The foundation of Dalit theology is built on the biblical truth that human beings are made in the image of God. This finds a familiar parallel with African American theologies. Rajkumar says that in a reconstruction of Dalit theology, one needs to be aware of the Hindu concept of the Brahman's body and the caste system's rejection of the Dalits, as distinct from the Body of Christ and the centrality of Jesus Christ. The recovery of the Dalit body as God's image in the church, as well as the body politic of the nation, is a challenge today.[10]

Another theologian, Dr. Monica Melanchthon, is one of the only two female Old Testament scholars in India holding a doctorate degree in the field. A widely sought-after international scholar, she teaches Old Testament in Gurukul Theological College, Chennai, India. She is also the head of the department of Women's Studies there. In an interview with her on January 8, 2004, she emphasized the dominant role of the Bible in the lives of women, both literate and non-literate.

Melanchthon spoke of the challenge of giving tools to women to reread the Bible. "The Bible is what I want to do," she said, emphasizing her role of teaching the Bible. "Women committed to the cause of women, consciously feminist, feminist in their orientation, can bring about change." She made the imperative clear: "Develop skills in women and equip women to reread the Bible from women's perspectives. That is what my calling seems to be." Melanchthon feels her role is more than "politicizing" the Dalit issue. It is "theologizing."

For Melanchthon, Indian Dalit women's hermeneutics, their interpretive tool, should be liberationist and liberative. Dalit women are referred to as "Dalits among Dalits." The hermeneutics should give liberation to Dalit women and offer liberation to all. She quotes John 10:10, where Jesus says that he has come to give fullness of life for all, the establishment of "shalom" for all.[11]

scriptures of other religious faiths should be treated with respect and with full acceptance, just as the Judaism of the Old Testament was incorporated into the Christian Gospel. Christians must go beyond their own traditional and inherited faith in order to discover God's ways. M. M. Thomas said that Christians needed to risk Christ for Christ's sake, and to take an active part in the daily struggles and activities of nation building in order to create a shalom community.

Subsequently, Indian theologians proposed radical changes in their approach to mission and ministry in post-independence India. One major paradigm shift was in the area of mission theology: to move from Christ-centered (Christocentric) theology to God-centered (theocentric) theology. They believed that while a God-centered approach would bring harmony and unity among the people of the world, a Christ-centered approach serves as a barrier.

Trying to be faithful to their Christian calling, they proposed several alternative models of mission theologies. The chart at right captures the differences between traditional theological thoughts and contemporary theological thoughts.

Dalit Theology

Dalit theology is a contextual theology, a counter-theology of the oppressed. It is a theology of identity and selfhood. It interprets the living experience of the Dalits in the light of the suffering, death, and resurrection of Jesus Christ. Such an interpretive attempt aims at transforming and empowering the Dalits who have been marginalized for generations.

Dalit theologians argue that traditional Indian theologians were preoccupied with the Hindu Brahminical traditions and failed to incorporate the voices of the Dalits. Therefore, the Dalits have to formulate their own theology, taking the death and suffering of Christ as a model. Jesus Christ was the prototype of all the Dalits and the Bible is a Dalit book, for it is a book of a people (the Hebrews) who were the social outcasts of the day and who lived "outside the camp."[12] Although the

Traditional and Contemporary Theological Thoughts

Traditional

Eurocentric
(Europe-centered)

Ecclesiocentric
(church-centered)

Christocentric
(Christ-centered)

Bibliocentric
(Bible-centered)

Soteriocentric
(salvation-centered)

Basileocentric
(kingdom-centered)

Otherworldly

Theology of New Testament

Ecumenicity of Denominations

Partnership with Other Denominations

Personal/Individual Salvation

Work for Personal Transformation

proponents of this theology are few in number, this theology has served as the bedrock for several Indian theologies such as women's theology and indigenous theology. It traces its origin to the South American theologian, Gustavo Gutierrez.

Indian Liberation Theology

Indian liberation theology argues that faith and praxis (action) go together: to know God is to love justice. Inherent in faith is the love of God that can be manifested in the love of one's neighbor. The struggles of the people against structures that dominate and oppress them must be taken into consideration while interpreting the scriptures and creating theologies.

Theology of Religious Pluralism

The proponents of this theology raise questions concerning the primacy of biblical texts and biblical canon. They argue that the sacred scriptures of other religions must be given places of respect. Christ should not be preached as "the only way." Christ is already present in other faiths, although hidden. If Christ becomes the center of mission theology, discussion, and engagement, it would exclude others. On the contrary, if God is made the center of all our mission activities and discussion, people of all religions could be brought together to serve the common good. A summary of this approach is that Christians should move from the Christ-centered approach of mission that alienates people of other faiths to a God-centered approach that includes all peoples. Many Christians in the pews, however, refuse to accept this view as it compromises their commitment to Christ. Many Christians in India would escape discrimination and persecution if they would subscribe to this theology.

Post-Colonial Theology

This theology is broad in approach and radical in stance. It rewrites the colonialists' understanding of mission and ministry in India, inviting Christians in India to move beyond biblical theology to local and contextual theology. By doing so, it incorporates local traditions as equally valid. It takes the oral and

Contemporary

Indocentric
(India-centered)

Local foci
(community-centered)

Theocentric
(God-centered)

Anthropocentric
(human-centered)

Shalomcentric
(shalom-centered)

Cosmocentric
(universal)

Earthly

Theology of Religious Pluralism

Ecumenicity of Religions

Companionship with Other Religions

Community/National Salvation

Work for Social Transformation

Students reciting the 23rd Psalm at Emmanuel Methodist School in Puduh, Chennai (Madras), India.

literal history, myths and stories, images and symbols of a people as equally authoritative and normative.

Women's Theology

Primarily based on liberating women from all forms of oppression, especially from under the subjugation of patriarchy, the perspective of women's theology is a response to and a challenge of traditional Christian theology based on Augustine's writings. These theologians argue that traditional theology is patriarchal and ignores women's experience. Women, primarily the rural and urban poor, indigenous, and Dalit women, are the victims of culturally sanctioned subjugation in India. These women are not only marginalized and exploited, but they are robbed of their human identity and selfhood. Through the ages both biblical and traditional theology have perpetuated the patriarchal attitude. Indian women are called to do theology by taking both the liberative texts of the Bible and the current context into consideration, and to search for egalitarian relationships and equal partnerships with men.

Indigenous Theology

Indigenous people are not stratified in the caste-based Hindu society, and their world view is different from that of other

Indian women are called to do theology by taking both the liberative texts of the Bible and the current context into consideration, and to search for egalitarian relationships and equal partnerships with men.

106

communities. For them, land is life and sustenance. Nature is their lifeline. Since their everyday experience is based on egalitarian and communal life, they call upon the larger Christian community to work actively for peace and justice with the indigenous people's world view in mind.

Theology of Harmony

The theology of harmony is a relatively new theology based on the Christian experience of dialogue with people of other faiths in a variety of life situations: action, faith, spirituality, beliefs, and practices. It strives to find a common meeting point and works toward peace and for the well-being of all people. The goal of this theology is to evolve an understanding of Christ as one who could bring all peoples together. This theology focuses on right relationships and how to live in peaceful coexistence.

CHALLENGES TO CHRISTIANS ON THE SUBCONTINENT AND THEIR THEOLOGIES

The Church in India

Since the vast majority of Indian Christians came from the poor and marginalized community with no economic and political clout, the call to engagement in nation-building is complicated by the lack of power and influence. Mainline Protestant churches are highly hierarchical, deeply institutionalized, and trenchantly middle class. There is a radical disconnect between mainline churches and independent congregations, which are more in number and made up of the economically disadvantaged.

Even though Christians in India make up about 3 percent of the population, a higher percentage of Indian Christians worship in churches on a given Sunday than do Christians in the West. Apart from denominational mission societies, the India Christian Mission Association is one of the largest self-sufficient organizations in the world. The mission societies under this broad umbrella organization are conservative in theology and evangelistic in outreach. Social transformation of communities

E ven though Christians in India make up about 3 percent of the population, a higher percentage of Indian Christians worship in churches on a given Sunday than do Christians in the West.

Interior of Lalbagh Methodist Church in Lucknow, India

Currently, about twenty thousand missionaries are supported by several missionary organizations within India, including the Indian Missionary Society and the Friends Missionary Band, that work under the India Mission Association. They send missionaries within India and abroad to work in cross-cultural contexts.

through mission engagement is often put on the back burner by a vast majority of the member organizations. Even those who are engaged in relief work are often confined to their own sites in which evangelistic work is done.

Currently, about twenty thousand missionaries are supported by several missionary organizations within India, including the Indian Missionary Society and the Friends Missionary Band, that work under the India Mission Association. They send missionaries within India and abroad to work in cross-cultural contexts.

Numerical growth continues to take place mainly among the poor and the marginalized communities through mass movements. In both the past and present, such mass conversions have taken place as movements of social protest against the Hindu caste system. Since Christianity affirms the dignity and equality of persons as disciples of Jesus Christ, many people from depressed communities, particularly the Dalit, join the church. Indian government agencies view these conversions with deep suspicion.

Rapid growth has also taken place among the Pentecostals and fundamentalists. Often they are passed over by mainline denominations, both Protestant and Catholic. A high degree of polarization exists between these two groups and other Christian groups.

Despite the guarantee the Indian Constitution provides for the total protection and complete equality of all citizens regardless of their religious affiliation, Christians in India face religious and socio-economic discrimination at the hands of Hindutva sectarians. Just as the Islamization of Pakistan (see Blasphemy Law, p. 112) is detrimental to religious minorities in Pakistan, Hinduization is detrimental to religious minorities in India. A politicized religion that claims a country exclusively for one religion is a threat to the social fabric of the land. A narrow concept of a religion spells danger to others.

A militant religious consciousness, Hindutva is the claim that India must be a Hindu nation and that the Hindus are the true children of the land. This narrow interpretation of Hinduism (see chapter 1) defines an alternative vision of India. The Supreme Court of India passed a judgement on December 11, 1995 saying:

> Ordinarily, Hindutva is understood as a way of life or state of mind, and it is not to be equated with, or understood as, religious Hindu fundamentalism.

A leading newspaper, *The Times of India*, responded, saying that the Court's opinion was "at variance with ground reality."[13] Bharatiya Janata, the former ruling party and organizations such as the Rashtriya Swayamsevak Sangh, the Shiv Sena, and Vishva Hindu Parishad stand for the ideology of Hindutva. True Hinduism is much broader and more tolerant than the ideology of Hindutva.

In 1992, extremist Hindus "reclaimed" the Hindu holy site at Ayodhya, birthplace of Rama, where a mosque was built.

Despite the guarantee the Indian Constitution provides for the total protection and complete equality of all citizens regardless of their religious affiliation, Christians in India face religious and socio-economic discrimination at the hands of Hindutva sectarians.

Children dressed as Hindu god Rama (right) and goddess Sita, attend the Kumbh Mela or "Great Fair," a sacred one-month festival in Nasik, India.

DEATH-DEALING INTERPRETA-
TIONS THAT INCITE
EXTREMISM NEED TO BE
CONFRONTED IN
ALL RELIGIOUS PRACTICES.

Sectarian riots in which Muslims were massacred broke out in the area, and riots erupted again in 2002. A leading newspaper, *The Hindu*, said, "Fear is today the dominant emotion in the lives of Gujarati Muslims."[14] The National Council of Churches in India and several other groups, including the International Initiative for Justice, raised the voice of advocacy on behalf of victims.[15]

It is imperative to prevent religion from "becoming a fault line between communities."[16] The life-giving traditions of religious texts need to be interpreted. Death-dealing interpretations that incite extremism need to be confronted in all religious practices. Traditions of peace-building and reconciliation within religions can be interfaith bridges.

In India, Hindu religious practices are incorporated by geopolitical powers and forces, which are, of course, secular. At times, the line between religion and the nation gets blurred and religious typologies get mixed. As a result, conflicts in the region could be simultaneously social and religious. Indian theology, especially mission theology, is often developed in the context of people of other faiths, but seldom defined as to how to confront raw power and justice denied. A prophetic voice in mission theology is slowly emerging.

A prophetic voice in mission theology is slowly emerging.

Indian theology is often placed in the context of Hinduism, but rarely in relation to Islam, Buddhism, and Sikhism, faiths which have totally different relationships with Christians. Indian mission theology primarily swirls around Christian-Hindu theology. However, one needs to bear in mind that the church in India is still a minority institution. It is politically powerless and communally vulnerable. Indian theology is shaped outside of the mainstream of organized and institutionalized structure. Christians face daily struggles against discrimination, intolerance, and hatred. They strive to remain faithful to their call as a church in the midst of oppression and marginalization. Resisting the temptation to be part of the majority in order to share its power and patronage, they must constantly define their self-identity and witness to their neighbors. Embracing weakness and powerlessness for the sake on one's faith may not make sense to those of us who are Christians in the West.

The Church in Pakistan

The Church of Pakistan was formed in 1970 as a result of the merger of Anglicans, Lutherans, Scottish Presbyterians, and Methodists. The Presbyterian Church of Pakistan, a separate denomination, relates to the Presbyterian Church (U.S.A.). The Church of Pakistan has eight dioceses, each with its own bishops. The dioceses of Multan and Raiwind are in those areas where Methodist work was done previously.

The Methodist Church was established in Pakistan in the 1800s, long before the partition of India. Initially begun as a mission to the English-speaking communities of Anglo-Indian and British military and civil personnel, the ministry was handed over to the British Wesleyan Methodist Church in 1900. In 1947, Pakistan became the first religious state in the world founded for majority Muslims. The Pakistani leadership gave its assurance to people of other faiths that they could practice their respective religions without hindrance.

Christians constitute about 3 percent of the population of Pakistan. The dioceses manage schools, hospitals, and community

Indian theology is often placed in the context of Hinduism, but rarely in relation to Islam, Buddhism, and Sikhism, faiths which have totally different relationships with Christians.

The Church of Pakistan was formed in 1970 as a result of the merger of Anglicans, Lutherans, Scottish Presbyterians, and Methodists.

centers that reach out not only to Christians, but also to the larger Muslim community. A former Bishop of the Diocese of Peshawar, Pakistan, and the General Secretary of the United Society for the Propagation of the Gospel, London, England, Bishop Munawar (Mano) Rumalshah, calls these places of ministry Diaconal Centers. The contribution of the churches, especially to health and education, is recognized by the government of Pakistan. The schools which were nationalized in 1972 have been returned to the churches.

The United Church of Pakistan has ordained two women. They are Khushnud Azariah, the former president of the World Federation of Methodist and Uniting Church Women, and Rohamah Asit, who teaches at St. Peter's School in Raiwind Diocese, Pakistan.

Blasphemy Law

Christians in Pakistan now practice "suffering Christianity" under the Islamization of the country. The introduction of a section of a penal code based on the Blasphemy Law that has been in existence for more than two centuries has created fear and panic among Christians for most of the last two decades. Pakistan's penal code, section 295-C reads:

> Whoever by words, either spoken or written or by visible representation, or by any imputation, innuendo, or insinuation, directly or indirectly, defiles the sacred name of the Holy Prophet Mohammed (PBUH) shall be punished with death, or imprisonment for life, and shall also be liable to fine.[17]

This well-intentioned law has often been abused as a tool for discrimination against religious minorities, including Christians, who have been victimized by this law. Bishop Rumalshah testified before the Senate Foreign Relations Committee in the United States on June 17, 1998, on "Being a Christian in Pakistan," relating the discriminations Christians face. He stated that the Blasphemy Law has been a "death wish" for many. However, he lifts up the hope of human dignity for the faith community when he says:

The United Church of Pakistan has ordained two women. They are Khushnud Azariah, the former president of the World Federation of Methodist and Uniting Church Women, and Rohamah Asit, who teaches at St. Peter's School in Raiwind Diocese, Pakistan.

Christians are sadly viewed to be the scum of the earth and our struggle is to give them a dignified living so that there may be truly gospel communities which are attractive. That is the struggle of the people and we continue to face those despite all the pressure we live under.[18]

He sees the role of Christians in the United States as "reconcilers." He states that if there is a "frontier situation for the church, it is in Pakistan," and asks that Christians in the United States live in a "tangible relationship" of prayer and support as part of the same "Body of Christ."[19]

> **Christians are sadly viewed to be the scum of the earth and our struggle is to give them a dignified living so that there may be truly gospel communities which are attractive.**

Mosque in Lahore, Pakistan

Food items being prepared for distribution at the Pakistan-Afghanistan border.

6

CHALLENGES AND OPPORTUNITIES, CELEBRATIONS AND ACTIONS

WHEN ONE KNOWS
THEE, THEN ALIEN THERE IS
NONE, THEN NO DOOR
IS SHUT. OH, GRANT ME MY
PRAYER THAT I MAY
NEVER LOSE THE BLISS OF THE
TOUCH OF THE ONE
IN THE PLAY OF THE MANY.

—GITANJALI RABINDRANATH TAGORE

This chapter explores some of the challenges inherent in economic globalization and privatization. It is also an invitation to celebrate some alternative visions of faith communities and non-government organizations for a more equitable world.

GLOBALIZATION: INFORMATION TECHNOLOGY

Globalization is a process by which the whole world is brought together in one huge supermarket of goods and services. In this global market economy, there is an increased flow of cross-border trade and investment. While there are opportunities for the flow of information, trade, and technology from one place to the other and for the global interdependence of goods and services, there are serious inequalities perpetuated by the process of globalization.

Transnational corporations make decisions with little or no regard for elected national governments. National economies are transformed into a single worldwide economy and governed by a single set of rules.[1] For the faith community, the realities of globalization raise some questions. Does the good of globalization outweigh the bad? Is globalization a phenomenon in which the good is the enemy of the best? Should we see the world as the household of God, or a marketplace?

Mission as development sees the world as *oikoumene*, the household of God, and people as stewards of the earth. Economic globalization sees the world as a marketplace, and people as consumers. When corporations influence governments and the latter adopt globalization as a strategy for economic development, then market forces rule the world.

Information technology is an example of economic globalization. India is one of the countries at the forefront of software technology. Bangalore's "Silicon Valley," the flood of software exports, and Hyderabad (often called Cyberabad) are some of India's technological centers.

Offshoring technology has become a recent trend just as offshoring manufacturing has been for decades. Offshoring companies to countries like India and China creates cheap high-tech labor pools there. Ashish Thadhani, an analyst at Brean Murray

AP/Wide World Photos

Professor Vijay Chandru of the Indian Institute of Science (left) displays the mother board of the Simputer, a cheap, handheld computer, as Vinay Deshpande, CEO of Encore software, shows the Simputer prototype in Bangalore, India on May 21, 2001.

Does the good of globalization outweigh the bad? Is globalization a phenomenon in which the good is the enemy of the best? Should we see the world as the household of God, or a marketplace?

> Market forces determine the flow of work in industries such as the garment and footwear industries, as well as producers of electronics. These unskilled labor pools are principally made up of women.

Student plowing field at Agricultural Institute in Allahabad, India

Research, says that General Electric saves $340 million a year by hiring 20,000 employees in India.[2] Outsourcing increasingly supplants jobs not only in the technology industry but also in fields such as accounting, law, and corporate business. This has led to some protectionist measures, legislative and otherwise, in states such as Connecticut and New Jersey.[3]

Some economists see profit in the practice of offshoring. U.S. companies hire companies in India and China and use them as call centers. Profits flow from these job flights. Globalization is at work creating cheap intellectual labor pools, pitting Americans against Indians. In India, the economic gap between the highly skilled high-tech employees and those who suffer under chronic poverty is ever widening.

Feminization of Labor and Poverty

Textiles and electronics companies employ the practice of subcontracting. This has led to what is known as the informal economy, where there is no unionized labor. Market forces determine the flow of work in industries such as the garment and footwear industries, as well as producers of electronics. These unskilled labor pools are principally made up of women.

Internal migration is a growing trend. When jobs are scarce, people move in search of work. As a result, there is a breakup of communities and a disintegration of the social fabric. Increasingly, the habitats of indigenous peoples are being destroyed by corporations in search of natural resources through mining, deforesting, and logging.

Privatization of Water

Water scarcity and population increasingly play into the hands of the privatization of water by corporations. The World Bank estimates that the water market has the potential of producing one trillion dollars. In certain places in India, it is easier to purchase Coca Cola or other soft drinks than clean water.

A leading Indian voice for ecological justice around the world is Dr. Vandana Shiva, the author of *Water Wars: Privatization, Pollution and Profit*. Through non-governmental organizations, she raises consciousness and holds governments responsible for exploiting ecological crises for economic benefits.

Rigid Identities

Lack of access to resources and power-sharing and being shut out of decision making may engender in people a sense of alienation and frustration, often resulting in violence. There are perceived and real threats to religious ways of life in communities. Increasing globalization, militarization, and the politicization of religions lead to rigid identities in people. Unfortunately, religions that should offer liberation from rigid and narrowly defined identities are often manipulated to polarize and further divide religious communities.

Bible Women: Border Crossings

Faith communities in the subcontinent continue to follow the alternative visions offered in the Bible for a world of shalom, healing, and wholeness. They continue to work on border crossings. One such instance is the work of the Bible Women.

Dating back to the nineteenth century, Bible Women are Christian workers recruited by missionaries from the early

Everything's discounted. Oceans, rivers, oil, gene pools, fig wasps, flowers, childhoods, aluminium factories, phone companies, wisdom, wilderness, civil rights, ecosystems, air, and all 4,600 million years of evolution.

—*Arundhati Roy*
The Friday Times, *Pakistan*
September 27–October 03, 2002
Vol. XIV, No. 31

The Women's Division revived the Bible Women Initiative in the year 2000. Today's Bible Women have been trained in India, Malaysia, Cambodia, the Philippines, and the Pacific Islands. In 2002, the Women's Division trained forty Bible Women in India in the Methodist Center in Chennai. The core training consisted of education in health and literacy, micro-credit and literacy, domestic violence, and HIV/AIDS.

women converts. Early female missionaries confronted a peculiar problem in their traditional host countries. Especially in India, they found that girls, on reaching puberty, were confined to and secluded in their homes.

The early missionaries found a way to circumvent patriarchy: they selected and trained native women who knew the culture and languages and possessed the ability to negotiate inside the secluded homes, often known as "zenanas." Zanana is the woman's part of the house, where women lived without exposure to the outside world. These women took the gifts of reading, writing, arithmetic, sewing, and home economics to the interiors of the secluded homes.

Bible Women laid the foundation for mission and evangelism among families and communities, especially in parts of the households reserved for female members. Bible Women trained local women and children in literacy and knowledge of the Bible. Learning to read the Bible in one's own language was the only literacy tool available to many Christian women in the mid-nineteenth century. Following the success of the model of Bible Women in India, missionaries employed this model in countries such as Japan, China, Korea, the Philippines, Taiwan, Malaysia, and Italy. Often Bible Women did the groundwork for the ministries of deaconesses. Today in India, there are 168 Methodist deaconesses.

The Women's Division revived the Bible Women Initiative in the year 2000. Today's Bible Women have been trained in India, Malaysia, Cambodia, the Philippines, and the Pacific Islands. In 2002, the Women's Division trained forty Bible Women in India in the Methodist Center in Chennai. The core training consisted of education in health and literacy, micro-credit and literacy, domestic violence, and HIV/AIDS.

Manuals on health and literacy and micro-credit and literacy are translated into Punjabi, Urdu, and Pashto, languages used in Pakistan. Plans by the Women's Division to train Bible Women in Pakistan are underway.

NON-GOVERNMENTAL ORGANIZATIONS

Non-governmental organizations demand accountability from governments and strive to strengthen the civil society. An example is the Centre for Legal Aid Assistance and Settlement (CLAAS) in Lahore, Pakistan. Begun in 1992 to address the issue of victimization and discrimination against religious minorities, women, and children, CLAAS offers free legal aid to those whose human rights are violated.[4]

DEALING WITH EXTREMISM

Vigilance is required to detect and address human rights violations that result from narrow interpretations of religions, including Christianity. Women Against Fundamentalisms is an organization launched in 1989 to challenge narrow interpretations of all religions.[5] The faith community also continues to raise its voices against religious intolerance and violence. In November 2002 the World Council of Churches sent a pastoral delegation to Pakistan. The aim was to address the issue of religious extremism. The WCC also sent letters of concern to the governments of India and Pakistan urging them to promote dialogues between religious communities and their governments.[6]

IMMIGRANTS AND THE AFTERMATH OF SEPTEMBER 11, 2001

Following the devastating attacks of September 11, 2001, fear has been a reality for many immigrant communities, especially immigrants from the Middle East and the Indian subcontinent. Fear among Pakistani immigrants stems in part from the massive arrests of people in what is known as "Little Pakistan" in Brooklyn. A story in the *Washington Post* (May 29, 2003) reported that out of the more than 120,000 Pakistanis who resided in "Little Pakistan," approximately 15,000 residents fled to Canada, Europe, and Pakistan soon after the event, according to Pakistani government estimates. According to the news account, federal

Following the devastating attacks of September 11, 2001, fear has been a reality for many immigrant communities, especially immigrants from the Middle East and the Indian subcontinent. Fear among Pakistani immigrants stems in part from the massive arrests of people in what is known as "Little Pakistan" in Brooklyn.

agents stopped and detained hundreds of Pakistanis in the aftermath of the attacks. After September 11, the Department of Homeland Security also required that every male Pakistani visa holder age sixteen or above register with the Bureau of Immigration and Customs Enforcement. Even now, Pakistani immigrants live under a cloud of suspicion.

The Patriot Act (HR. 3162), a key law passed on October 26, 2001, was designed to deter and punish terrorist acts in the United States and around the world and to enhance law enforcement investigatory tools. While terrorists must be brought to justice, the balance between security and civil rights was at stake because of the arrests of innocent immigrants. At this writing, some remain incarcerated, secluded from family and friends, and without due process of law.

The Patriot Act II calls for an extension of law enforcement powers at the expense of privacy and civil liberties, among them issuing subpoenas without having to show probable cause, and denying bail to anyone accused of domestic or international terrorism. A bipartisan group of lawmakers and advocacy groups has been working on achieving a balance between security and freedom. Many advocacy groups, such as "Not In My Town," an organization dedicated to racial justice, are engaged in addressing stereotyping, racial-profiling, and discrimination against Pakistani immigrants.

The Women's Division has also urged United Methodist Women to work for the establishment of civil liberties safe zones in their communities. As of May 2004, 320 communities in forty-one states had passed resolutions and ordinances to make their communities civil liberties safe zones. Fifty-one-and-a-half million people, that is, one in 5.5 U.S. residents, live in civil liberties safety zones.[7]

CROSS-RACIAL APPOINTMENTS IN THE UNITED METHODIST CHURCH

United Methodist ministers and their spouses from Pakistan and India serve in large and small communities across the country in cross-cultural and cross-racial appointments. To a male pastor from India or Pakistan, to serve in a cross-racial appointment evokes the metaphor of a double twist and a perfect landing in figure skating. For women, it could be likened to a triple twist and a perfect landing.

At the same time, for a local church to have a minister from some other part of the world is an act of border crossing. Many ministers from the developing world have seen the phenomenal growth of the Christian churches in their countries of origin. Therefore, they bring additional global Christian perspectives to their ministries.

By opening themselves to such appointments, local churches and annual conferences in the United States engage in and experience a ministry of mutuality and partnership. Cross-racial and cross-cultural appointments are a visible demonstration of crossing barriers and borders, such as East and West, and seeking to build one great family, the Body of Christ.

SOUTH ASIAN YOUTH: LEADERSHIP BUILDING

The General Board of Global Ministries has sponsored conferences in 2003 and 2004 for South Asian youth in the United States. Some of the issues addressed were identity as South

Street scene in Mumbai (Bombay), India

To a male pastor from India or Pakistan, to serve in a cross-racial appointment evokes the metaphor of a double twist and a perfect landing in figure skating. For women, it could be likened to a triple twist and a perfect landing.

Marisa Villarreal

Asians, empowerment, Christian networking, South Asian Christian culture, and inter-generational understanding.

Naming the problem of South Asian youth as an endless "struggle with their place in the church and society," the leadership of South Asian Youth has adopted as its mission statement, "to develop and fortify South Asian youth leadership," and to succeed in "reaching out and understanding generations and new youth immigrants." Their aim is to achieve a "strong Christian Network." [8]

EXCHANGE AND COMPANIONSHIP

Clement John, originally from Pakistan and working with the World Council of Churches, says,

> There is an exchange of journalists and professional people between Pakistan and India. The churches should take the lead and support the exchange of church people between India and Pakistan. [9]

The churches should take the lead and support the exchange of church people between India and Pakistan. [9]

Southeast Asia Youth Conference, outside of Chicago, Illinois, July 2003

Glory Dharmaraj

Accompaniment of peoples across the borders is a missional need.

Frances Major, a former missionary to India who has undertaken several trips to India since her retirement in 1989, felt that Volunteers in Mission projects should be utilized more by The

Elaine Magalis

Street scene, Mumbai (Bombay), India

WE NEED TO WALK WITH PEOPLE. I HAVE ADOPTED THE WORD, 'COMPANIONSHIP,' NOT PARTNERSHIP. WE ARE JUST THERE TO UNDERSTAND. THIS IS A MISSION FOR THE U.S.A. TODAY.[10]

United Methodist Church, especially by United Methodist Women, in order to promote better understandings with Pakistan and India, saying:

> We need to walk with people. I have adopted the word, 'companionship,' not partnership. We are just there to understand. This is a mission for the U.S.A. today.[10]

As faith communities, our call is to be co-creators with God, giving rise to a world of healing and wholesomeness. Let us celebrate our dual calling: to be faithful members of Christ's Body, and to be responsible stewards in the world, which is the household of God. Collectively and individually, let us continue to look for clues for social change, work on action plans, and celebrate our ongoing efforts at companionship and accompaniment, as mission endeavors.

Collectively and individually, let us continue to look for clues for social change, work on action plans, and celebrate our ongoing efforts at companionship and accompaniment....

EPILOGUE:
"GIVE THE AMERICAN PEOPLE MY LOVE"

Heaven forbid people should forget I played Gandhi.

—Sir Ben Kingsley, Oscar winning lead character in "Gandhi"

At the end of World War II, just before India and Pakistan got their freedom, E. Stanley Jones remarked to Gandhi that he was going back to America on a visit. The gist of their conversation follows, from Jones' *Gandhi: Portrayal of a Friend*:

Jones: Can you give me a message to the American people?

Gandhi: I have not seen the American people, but give them my love.

Jones went on to say that it was not a "sentimental love," but a love that Gandhi would give to even the people against whom he fought for freedom, the British. Jones went on to reflect on this message of Gandhi:

Suppose we should as a people—American, British, all—send our love to the world in terms something like these: We send you our love. And we mean it. We have no quarrel with your people. We know that you hate and fear war as we hate and fear war. We do not want to march out our young men against your young men in needless, senseless mass slaughter. We have no desire to conquer your country or any other country. We believe you have the same right to work out your destiny as we to work out ours. We hope and believe that you will reciprocate our love. If so, then war will be impossible between us, no matter what our political leaders say or do. But if a senseless madness would seize us and we should again go into war, out of which both would emerge ruined, but one a little stronger so that he would be called the conqueror, we would still not be hopeless. If you would be the conqueror, we should return to our senses and apply non-violent resistance. Our spirit would not allow you to conquer us—for long. We should conquer you with new weapons—weapons which would strengthen us and weaken you as they were applied. But if we should conquer you in a senseless military war, then we hope that you in turn would apply to us this same non-violent resistance. In that case you would save your freedom—and us. For in conquering you we should put ourselves in bondage to hold you down. We do not want to hold anybody down. We want everybody to be free everywhere. We send you our love—and mean it.[1]

Then Jones asks a poignant question: "Suppose they won't take love?"

Suppose they would not take love? Is that not the risk at the heart of God? God so *loved* the world that God took a risk, the risk called Jesus.

"Give them my love."

"Suppose they won't take it?"

It is an act worth risking in both public and private spheres. In the twenty-first century, it is our mission to rediscover this love—love in its daring simplicity and all its risk.

"Give them my love."

"Suppose they won't take it?"

INDIA & PAKISTAN
A MISSION STUDY
FOR 2005—2006

A STUDY GUIDE

FORWARD

For decades Schools of Christian Mission have been informing people about a variety of issues and places and challenging them to respond with action plans or changes in their lives to reflect their commitment to God's call for their lives. I am a woman whose worldview and concepts of mission have been formed by Schools of Christian Mission. I attended my first SOCM in 1980 and was hooked. The in-depth studies, the invitation to learn, the wealth of resources and approaches, the study leaders, and the awareness that I was part of a group of committed Christians who were addressing complex issues were stimulating and challenging. I also found that the background information and approaches dovetailed with the projects I worked on with gifted students in issue debates, environmental competitions, Model UNs, and geography fairs. What a great way to continue my education as I was growing in my awareness of The United Methodist Church at work in our world.

The 2005–2006 geographic study is timely and complex. India and Pakistan are often at odds, but once they were one country. They have a vastly varied and complex religious composition in which Christians are a minority community. We have an immense challenge to understand these issues and a greater challenge to be involved in India and Pakistan in Christian mission. This study is an opportunity to dig deep and to learn about our neighbors in India and Pakistan—from their ancient history and fascinating culture to current justice issues. Indian and Pakistani Christians have a powerful witness to share with us. This study is an opportunity to hear those stories (individually or in small groups) and to listen for God's call in our lives. What are we being called to do in response to what we are learning?

INTRODUCTION

The overall goals of this study are for each participant and group:

- to examine religious and historical events that have formed the modern day nations of India and Pakistan;

- to describe and appreciate aspects of contemporary life in India and Pakistan;

- to understand the conflicts that exist within and between the countries of India and Pakistan;

- to strengthen Christian witness through faithful partnership.

Schools of Christian Mission provide a challenging arena in which to learn together. In regional schools you will have four two-hour class sessions combined with a plenary experience and additional exhibits and resources.

Conference schools and events range from a short overview to four two-hour class sessions.

District and local church events also range from a one-session "program" to a longer study. Offer this study over a period of weeks for the whole church or in a church school class. One congregation (Grace United Methodist Church) offers four two-hour Sunday evening sessions culminating in a covered dish dinner the final evening. They call the experience "Grace University."

Check with your dean or the person in charge to find out your schedule and modify the lessons according to your needs. Your dean (or another member of the school committee) will be able to tell you what audio-visual resources will be available to you and what kind of a classroom setup you will have.

Questions to Consider:

Whether you are teaching in a four-day School of Christian Mission (four two-hour sessions), a shorter mission event, a district mission event, or a local church experience, begin by asking the following questions:

• How many class sessions will we have?

• How long are the class sessions?

• How many participants will be in the class?

• Are there chalkboards, dry erase boards, newsprint, bulletin boards, and other equipment in the classroom?

• Do you have the option of using PowerPoint or videos? Can the room be darkened? Is there an LCD projector and screen? Is there a TV/VCR available for your use?

• Are there tables you can use to display books and artifacts?

• Is there a table that can be used for creating a worship center?

• Will you be sharing your room with other groups?

• Is the room secure so that you can leave your displays and materials out for the duration of the study? What needs to be taken down and put up at the end and beginning of each class?

• Are there other study leaders for the India/Pakistan study? If so, you may be able to set up common displays or offer combined class video showings. You may also want to discuss your plans together. Sharing ideas and the individual gifts of leaders can enrich the experience for everyone.

• Will the participants have access to the Internet? (If not, you may want to download and print relevant website information in advance.)

Advance Preparation:

• Be in prayer for yourself and for your class participants.

• Read the complete text and study guide.

• If you have the option, contact class participants via mail or e-mail a few weeks before the first class session. Introduce yourself and ask that they join you in praying for the preparations that are being made for this study. Ask that they also begin to look for newspaper or magazine articles focusing on India or Pakistan. Request that they bring some symbol of India or Pakistan to class with them. This might be a memento from a trip, something that was produced in one of those countries, a book, a picture, some food to share, and so forth. If they have time, they might order the study book and get a head start on reading it. It can be ordered from the Service Center at 1-800-305-9857.

• Pull together your own collection of India/Pakistan memorabilia, posters, maps, and other materials to create an interesting and stimulating visual learning space.

• Order any audio-visual resources that you will use. Allow enough time for the resources to get to you.

• Other resources you will need include Bibles, *The United Methodist Hymnal*, *Global Praise I*, *New World Outlook*, and *Response* magazines, and the 2005 Mission Study Map on India and Pakistan.

- The websites listed are for additional information and are optional. If you wish for your participants to do a project using one of the suggested sites and Internet access is not available, arrange to download and print the relevant material and bring it to class as hard copy.

Classroom Setup:

- **Displays:** On the walls or bulletin boards, display maps, photos of Indian scenes, and quotations from Appendix C, Quotable Quotes (p. 169). Check teacher supply stores for posters and pictures.

- **Action Board:** Set up an action board or display a piece of newsprint so that participants can list ways of responding to the study daily, both during brainstorming sessions and as participants take their breaks.

- **Worship Center:** Set up a worship center for the duration of the study.

  - **If possible, cover a table with batik cloth**, particularly appropriate because the process may have originated in India. Batik is an ancient process of using melted wax to coat a design prior to dipping fabric into a cold water dye. The initial wax is removed and reapplied, another darker color is added, and the process is repeated until the desired effect is achieved. If batik is not available, use a solid color tablecloth.

  - **Include a cross, an open Bible, and a small globe.**

  - **Add other objects** to symbolize aspects of Indian or Pakistani life as the study progresses. The symbol might be chosen by the class for inclusion on the worship table next day.

  - **Rice and wheat or Indian bread:** Rice is the staple grain of southern India; wheat is the staple grain of northern India and Pakistan.

  - **Spices typical of Indian/Pakistani food:** Typical Indian spices are curries which include coriander, turmeric, cumin seed, fenugreek, black pepper, and cayenne or chili pepper.

  - **Picture of an Indian or Pakistani child:** To put a face on the people of the subcontinent, especially the most vulnerable.

  - **Pitcher of water:** The majority of the population of Pakistan does not have access to potable water. Control of water is also a border issue between India and Pakistan. The heavy rains associated with the monsoons of India can be both life threatening and life giving.

  - **Candles and small terra cotta lamps:** A part of many religious festivals in India, they can symbolize the culture of India.

  - **Flower garlands:** Flowers are used as decorations for Indian and Pakistani celebrations.

Options for Teaching:

This study guide includes four two-hour sessions, with a selection of exercises and learning options. Pick and choose the options that match your strengths and meet the needs of your class members. Feel free to adapt the exercises to suit your situation. Consider a team approach. Enlist the help of teenagers, friends with specific gifts, or volunteers from the class to read, act, sing, and so forth.

- Always debrief an exercise.
- Incorporate some of your own informational presentations.

- Invite someone from India or Pakistan to join the class for a portion of a session.
  - Use the Oprah Winfrey approach: interview the person, then allow questions from the class.
  - Ask the person to demonstrate how to do something from their ethnic background (dress someone in a sari, decorate someone with henna, demonstrate how to make an Indian or Pakistani recipe, teach the class some common words, share about their religion, share their story of coming to America).

Multiple Intelligence Theory:

Current educational research suggests incorporating a variety of approaches to any educational effort. Howard Gardner uses the term multiple intelligences to describe eight ways of learning, and suggests using a variety of teaching approaches to address those learning preferences: verbal presentations; problem solving; visualizing through pictures, maps, and diagrams; hands-on activities and simulations; using music; group discussion and interaction with others; tuning in to nature. The study sessions include a wide variety of exercises and options for you to enhance the time you have with your class.

Appendices:

Included in this text are:

- **Appendix A, Indian and Pakistani Recipes** that might be used as a treat for your class or for a church dinner.

- **Appendix B, Crossword Puzzle** with clues of chapter numbers or sections of the study guide where you'll find the answers. Crossword puzzle addicts learn a lot of extraneous material as they search for words to match given clues.

- **Appendix C, Quotable Quotes** with quotations that could be used on bulletin boards or walls or in some of the discussion exercises.

- **Appendix D, Time Lines** with relevant dates for the subcontinent as well as parallel dates in world and U.S. history.

- **Appendix E, For the Fun of It**, with suggestions for additional activities that can be found on the Internet.

- **Appendix F, Religious Smarts**, with instructions for a game.

- **Appendix G, Voices from Kashmir**, a simulated panel presentation.

- **Appendix H, Quotations from Holy Books**, with quotations from the holy scriptures of other faiths.

- **Appendix I, Documentary Special on India & Pakistan: Class Tasks,** a list of suggested elements for a simulated documentary.

- **Appendix J, A Dialogue Between Isabella Thoburn and Clara Swain**, an imaginary dialogue between two mission pioneers.

One-Session Study

Materials and Supplies:

- Bibles
- copies of *The United Methodist Hymnal*
- copies of this text
- copies of *Response* and *New World Outlook* magazines
- newsprint, markers, and tape
- TV and VCR or LCD projector

Preparation:

1. Read through the suggestions for this session and decide which option(s) you will use. If you are inviting a speaker, be sure the invited speaker understands the audience being addressed and the time constraints (whatever time you have determined for the presentation, plus time for questions). Have enough conversations with your speaker that you get a sense of his/her story. Are there issues that were covered in the book that your speaker might comment on? Plan to monitor the time and serve as moderator for the discussion.

2. If you choose to have magazine article reviews presented, give volunteers appropriate copies of *Response* and *New World Outlook*. With a book review, give the reviewer the book in plenty of time for reading and preparation.

3. If you choose to show a video, order the video well in advance and make sure the needed equipment is available to you.

Opening Worship (10 minutes):

Choose one of the times of opening worship and Bible study found in the session plans.

Getting Acquainted (20 minutes):

Divide participants into small groups of three or four. Ask them to introduce themselves within their small groups and respond to the following:

– What images come to mind when you think of India or Pakistan?

– What news have you heard recently that relates to India or Pakistan?

Present the Topic (35 minutes):

Some options for one program include:

1. **Invite a speaker from India or Pakistan.** Is there a pastor in your conference or district from India or Pakistan? You might handle this like a talk show host and prepare a set of questions or suggestions, such as the following:

   – Tell us about yourself and how you came to be in the United States.

   – Is there an Indian or Pakistani community here that you can relate to?

   – What ethnic customs and traditions do you try to maintain?

   – What's been most difficult in the transition from India/Pakistan to America?

2. **Invite a speaker who can focus on mission work** in India/Pakistan.

3. **Ask several persons to prepare short presentations** on the issues raised in the study that they found most interesting or that seem most relevant to your situation.

4. **Ask several people to review articles** related to India/Pakistan in *Response* and *New World Outlook*.

5. **Use the video and suggested questions** for discussion from the 2005 Mission Studies Video.

6. **Use one or more of the videos,** *Stolen Childhoods* (*www.stolenchildhoods.org*), *When Children Do the Work*, and *One Child's Labor*, from Session 4 of the study guide (page 157).

Discussion (20 minutes):

Depending on the type of presentation you have had, allow for discussion time and actions your group might take in response to what they have heard. Plan to serve as moderator for the discussion. Include the following questions:

   – What does it mean to be a neighbor?

   – What impact does the Patriot Act have on immigrants?

Closing Prayer (5 minutes):

Choose one of the closing prayers in the session plans.

Intergenerational Covered Dish Dinner

Many people will never have the option of traveling to India or Pakistan, but they would love to experience those cultures in the comfort of their own church. An intergenerational covered dish dinner is a way to enable this to happen. This is also a way to wrap up a churchwide study on India and Pakistan.

Materials and Supplies:

- garlands, poster, and maps for decorations (see Preparation)
- mission projects displays (see Preparation)
- Bibles
- copies of *The United Methodist Hymnal*
- resources needed for program (see Preparation)
- newsprint and easel, markers, and tape

Preparation:

1. Connsider working with a committee to plan decorations and set up displays. Public or private school teachers are often a good resource for additional creative ideas for presentations or hands-on activities, as well as for sources for photographs, maps, and other visuals.

2. Well in advance of the event, photocopy and give selected cooks the "Indian and Pakistani Recipes" in Appendix A (p. 162), so that the food selections can include tastes of India and Pakistan.

3. Set up displays that focus on mission projects in India and Pakistan. Use posters and maps from the packet provided by the United Methodist Children's Fund for Christian Mission *(http://gbgm-umc.org/global_news/full_article.cfm?articleid=1434)* and UMCOR Emergency kits—school kits, sewing kits, health kits, layettes, and bedding paks *(http://gbgm-umc.org/umcor/kits.cfm)*.

4. From colored poster board, make placards for each table. On one side, print the name of one

of the mission projects in India/Pakistan. On the other, print the following:

– What images come to mind when you think of India or Pakistan?

– What news have you heard recently that relates to India or Pakistan?

If you are using round tables, one placard per table is enough. For rectangular tables, you may need two or three placards per table.

5. For decorations, use lots of flower garlands (see Appendix E, "For the Fun of It," p. 174, for website addresses that include instructions for making flower garlands). Children's church school classes might help create the garlands. Also check at teacher supply stores for travel posters, maps, and other visuals.

6. If you plan to use a video, locate a VCR and an LCD projector and screen. If you have a media center located in the sanctuary, make arrangements to move the group there for the program.

Arrival Activity:

As they arrive, invite participants to look over the displays.

Table Talk (5 minutes):

Ask people to introduce themselves around their tables and use the questions on their placard as conversation prompts for talking about India/Pakistan with those sitting near them.

Opening Worship (10 minutes):

Open with worship using the devotions outlined for Session 3 in the study guide. When asked, "What institutions or ministries supported by the United Methodist Church take away the burdens of the bent-over people of India and Pakistan?" people can respond with the mission projects named at their tables.

Program (30 minutes):

Have a presentation as suggested in the One-Session Study.

Discussion (10 minutes):

Tailor the discussion time to the kind of presentation made. Ask the group to consider how your congregation might respond to what they've heard. List those suggestions on newsprint for follow up later.

Closing Prayer (5 minutes):

Close with one of the prayers from the four-session study or a prayer of your own.

Four-Session Study
Session

Objectives:

1. To be introduced to the study of India and Pakistan.

2. To discover what the group knows of India and Pakistan and to correct misinformation and misunderstandings about both countries.

3. To explore the relationship between ancient history and beliefs and the current attitudes of the people of the subcontinent.

Materials and Supplies:

• Different colored markers, newsprint, and easel (or dry erase board and dry erase markers)

• Bibles

• copies of *The United Methodist Hymnal*

• prepared slips of paper and a small container or basket (see Preparation)

• assumptions printed on newsprint (see Preparation)

• two copies of the 2005 Mission Study Map of India and Pakistan (or photocopies of the information on the back of the map)

Preparation:

1. If the number of class participants is between eighteen and thirty, set up chairs in groups of six (if the class number is smaller or larger, arrange chairs for small discussion groups of three to six people and choose portions of the exercises for the number of groups you have). Make enough slips of paper with the numbers one through six (or a number for each group you will have) so that each participant will have a slip. Designate sections in the room or groups of chairs for each number. Place the slips of paper in a small container or basket.

2. Print the word "Namaste" on the chalkboard or dry erase board, or on a sheet of newsprint. Practice saying the word, pronounced **Na ma stay.**

3. Also print the Sharing Assumptions, listed on this page, on newsprint and display them.

4. Look over "Sarinam, Sarinam" (*The United Methodist Hymnal*, #523). Enlist a pianist to play the hymn. Go over the hymn until you are familiar with it. If you are not comfortable singing, enlist a musician who can help teach the hymn to your group.

5. If you decide to use "Fill My Cup, Lord," note that the version printed in *The United Methodist Hymnal* includes only the refrain, not the verses. If you would like to sing the verses, you can find the words and hear how the melody sounds online at *http://www.jesusone.com/dailyhymn/fillmycuplord.htm* or *http://www.barbcoolwaters.com/713a051.html*. In advance, ask one of the participants who is a singer to practice singing the verses.

6. Display the 2005 Mission Study Map of India and Pakistan and the information from the back of the map.

Arrival Activities (10 minutes):

As participants arrive, have them draw one of the slips of paper and go to the small group area in the classroom that is designated for that number.

Sanskrit Greeting:

Greet your class members with an Indian greeting pressing your hands together and holding them near your heart with your head gently bowed as you say, "Namaste," (pronounced **Na ma stay**). Say:

In Sanskrit, "Namas" means "bow," a reverential salutation. "Te" means "to you." So "namaste" means "I bow to you." This is both a spoken greeting and a gesture, a Mantr(a) and a Mudr(a). The prayerful hand position is called Anjali, meaning "to honor."

Sharing Assumptions:

Call participants' attention to the assumptions you printed on newsprint:

• We are partners in the learning experience—neither the study leader nor any class member will dominate.

• We will listen to each other with respect.

• We have the right to "pass" on any exercise.

• Because there is much material to cover, we will limit reports to the class, exercises, and discussions according to time schedules set by the study leader.

• Learning takes place when we commit to read the text; to prepare outside of class; to reflect together on issues and on what we believe; to participate in the suggested exercises.

Introductions (10 minutes):

Introduce yourself. Depending upon the size of your class, ask participants to introduce themselves in either the small groups or in the total group, and share the following (remind them to be brief):

– *In a School of Christian Mission*, their name and home church; *in a local church group*, some concern they carry to class with them.

– Any particular knowledge or experience of India or Pakistan; something they've heard in the news recently about India or Pakistan.

– Symbols of India/Pakistan. These can be placed around the class on the walls and tables.

– What they hope to get out of this class.

Opening Worship (20 minutes):

Bible Study and Reflection:

Ask for a volunteer to read John 4:7-15 as the participants follow along in their Bibles.

Read the following, or put it in your own words:

Although many who read this passage of scripture focus on the woman's sin or Jesus's willingness to talk to a woman, this narrative is also about belief in Jesus by a religiously ostracized group. Over and over in the New Testament we find Jesus relating to Samaritans in ways that were outside Jewish standards. Jews were not to associate with Samaritans in any way. Jesus interacted with them, and even used them as positive examples in some of his parables.

From ancient times in India the Aryans divided society into castes. Within this classed society, the Dalits were assigned the most menial tasks (cleaning and removing dirt, removing waste, tanning animal hides, and taking care of dead bodies). Considered "untouchable," the Dalits were outside the realm of society. Those in other castes did not touch them, talk with them, eat with them, or have any social connection with them. Those ancient beliefs persist in parts of India today. Listen to the voice of a Dalit woman.

Ask for a volunteer to read "The Story of a Dalit Woman" (sidebar, pp. 84-85).

In their small groups, have participants discuss the following:

– What are the parallels between Jewish attitudes towards Samaritans and the ancient and still-existing attitudes towards the Dalits within India?

– Who are the Dalits/Samaritans in our society?

– When have you felt like an outsider?

– What are we called to do to remedy the situation?

Hymn Singing:

Teach the group and Indian hymn, "Saranam, Saranam" (*The United Methodist Hymnal*, #523). If you like, also sing "Fill My Cup, Lord" (*The United Methodist Hymnal*, #641), either just the refrain as printed in the hymnal, or the verses too if you arranged to have someone sing them.

Prayer:

Pray the following, or a prayer of your own:

O God, who breaks down barriers and brings reconciliation, forgive us when we preserve the walls and barricades of pride, privilege, and tradition. Give us compassion for those whose paths are different, or whose race or language or culture is different from our own. Give us the grace to prize the differences, and to appreciate the unique gifts you give to others. Forgive the many ways we separate ourselves, and give us a welcoming Spirit, that we may offer the good news of Christ to all we meet. Amen.

Geographic Awareness (20 minutes):

Ask that each small group designate a discussion leader to make sure each person has an opportunity to share and no one dominates the discussion. Each small group should also designate a reporter to report back to the whole group.

Assign to each of the small groups one of the assignments below. Direct the groups to explore their topic using the maps in the book, the 2005 Mission Study Map of India and Pakistan, and the information from the back of the map.

Group 1: Name the countries that border India and Pakistan. From the time line in Appendix D (p. 172), or your own knowledge, can you find any information on alliances after WWII with other countries or hostilities between any of these countries?

Group 2: Which major rivers flow through India and Pakistan? What are some Indian/Pakistani environmental/water issues?

Group 3: Locate and identify the capital cities of India and Pakistan. Also locate in India: Mumbai (until recently known as Bombay), Calcutta (the largest metropolis in India), Hyderabad (a vital center of Islamic culture in India), and in Pakistan: Karachi (the largest metropolis in Pakistan), and Lahore.

Group 4: What are some languages spoken in India? Note: Children in India learn at least three languages in school. What languages are spoken in Pakistan? What challenges face these countries where multiple languages are spoken?

Group 5: Identify the major trading partner of India and Pakistan. Obtain some economic information for each country.

Group 6: Find the literacy rate for India and Pakistan. What differences do you find between the literacy rate for males and females in each country?

When groups have had about five minutes to work, ask each group report their findings briefly to the entire class.

Human Population Graph (30 minutes):

Ask class members to consider what it means to be in the majority or minority position.

Information sharing (source: *http://www.adherents. com/Religions_By_Adherents.html*). Say:

If the people in this room represented the peoples of the world,

- one out of every six of you would be Chinese (16.7 percent),
- one would be Indian (16.7 percent);
- four (66 percent) would represent the rest of the world.

Therefore, one of our small groups represents the people of China, one represents the people of India, and the other four groups represent the rest of the world.

Ask participants to consider the following:

– The United States has less than one third the number of people in either China or India.

– The United States spends the most money on its military—more than the next twelve nations combined.

Now ask participants to shift their mental image to religious affiliations. Say:

If the people in this classroom represented the religious people of the world:

- **33 percent would be Christian** (point to two of the groups and designate them Christian);
- **22 percent would be Muslim** (point to one of the groups and designate them Muslim);
- **15 percent would be Hindu** (point to one of the groups and designate them Hindu);
- **16 percent would be the rest of the religions of the world** (point to one of the groups and designate them other religions);
- **14 percent would be secular, nonreligious,**

agnostic, or atheist (point to the last group and designate them to be in this category).

Then say:

Now imagine you are all citizens of Pakistan (to simplify the human graph, have the participants in one of the groups distribute themselves evenly into the other groups).

• **97 percent of you are Muslim (77 percent Suni, 20 percent Shi'a)**;

• **3 percent of you are Christian**.

That means that four of our five groups are made up of Suni Muslims and one group is populated with Shi'a Muslims. Christians, Hindus, and any other religions wouldn't be counted at all on our human graph unless we had thirty-three bodies. Then we could pull one from the Suni Muslim area and label that person Christian.

Imagine you are now all citizens of India.

• **83 percent of the people living in India are Hindu** (designate four of the five groups Hindu).

• **The fifth group will be Muslim** (14 percent), Christians (3 percent), and other smaller religious minorities (Sikhs, Jains, Buddhists, Jews, Parsis, Ahmadi, and Bah).

Remind the class that India has over a billion people. The Institute of Islamic Information and Education suggests that 14 percent of the Indian population is Muslim, (nearly 145 million Muslims), even more than Pakistan (approximately 140 million). When you consider the huge population of India, Christians (3 percent) would number 30 million.

Give the original small groups a few minutes to discuss the following questions (on newsprint or the board):

– What are some of the issues facing Christians living in India or Pakistan?

– What issues face Muslims living in India, or Hindus living in Pakistan?

Ask the small groups to report to the total group.

Alternative Activity:

If the class is not large enough to have six small groups, gather around a table where you have divided 100 pennies into six groups based on the percentages above. Ask the following:

– What would be important to know about Indian and Pakistani ancient history?

– Why? (One possible answer: to be aware of the foundations of a culture; to gain an understanding of why some attitudes are so difficult to change, e.g., the attitude towards Dalits in India.)

Quick Response (5 minutes):

Ask the following:

– What do you already know or think you know about the ancient history of Pakistan and India? (Record on newsprint or the board.)

Small Group Reading Exercise (15 minutes):

Have the six small groups read the section of the chapter that connects to the following points. Ask groups to determine the main points of the reading and assign someone to report to the rest of the class.

1. The Aryan Invasion (p. 16)

2. The Impact of Ancient Hindu Society and Writings (p. 17)

3. Ancient History, Writings, and Caste (p. 19)

4. Ancient History, Writings, and the Role and Status of Women (p. 20)

5. Ancient History, Writings, and Politics (p. 21)

6. Romanticizing Ancient History and Writings (p. 22)

Sharing with the Total Group (5 minutes):

As the reporters share, use a different color marker to correct or add to the list of what the group knows about the ancient history of India.

Responsive Reading on East-West Philosophy (optional):

Ask two volunteers to read "East-West Philosophy in a Nutshell" (pp. 24-26). Or divide the group into two groups and read it responsively.

Closing (5 minutes):

Reading:

Have a volunteer read Schreiter's "Seven Ways to Distinguish the Other" (sidebar, p. 23).

Hymn Singing:

Sing together "In Christ There is No East or West" (*The United Methodist Hymnal*, #548). Also sing "Saranam, Saranam" (*The United Methodist Hymnal*, #523).

Pray Together:

Invite participants to read in unison the following prayer:

Lord, we are grateful for the amazing beauty of your world and the people you have created. Help us affirm the uniqueness of all your children. Guide us as we learn more about our brothers and sisters in India and Pakistan. Enable us to learn from them. Give us the grace to accept our differences and the compassion to be in solidarity with those who are plagued with injustice. Help us discover ways to serve you in India and Pakistan. Open our hearts and our minds, O Lord, that we might discern how you want us to respond to what we learn in this study. Amen.

Assignment:

Write the following on the chalkboard, dry erase board, or on a sheet of newsprint:

• Ask participants to read chapters 2 and 3 from the text.

• Ask for one volunteer to read/act out Clorinda's Story (p. 42), and for three volunteers for the Kashmir panel (Voices from Kashmir, Appendix G, p. 179).

• Have students pick out the class tasks they will do for the final session (Documentary Special on India/Pakistan: Class Tasks, Appendix I, p. 184).

Session

2

Objectives:

1. To examine the role that religion plays in India and Pakistan.

2. To explore what forced the British to give up their rule over India.

3. To consider the role that Gandhi played in acquiring India's freedom from British rule and how his methodology influenced others worldwide.

4. To become aware of the dynamics of the creation of the nation of Pakistan.

5. To investigate the reasons for the current situation in Kashmir.

Materials and Supplies:

• copies of *The United Methodist Hymnal*

• *(optional)* copy of the 2003 mission study book *Creating Interfaith Community* by R. Marston Speight with study guide by Glory and Jacob Dharmaraj

• Bibles

• copies of Gandhi quotes (see Preparation)

• video or DVD of *Gandhi—the Salt March*, and VCR or DVD player and TV

• chalkboard and chalk or dry erase board and dry erase markers or newsprint, markers, and tape

• prepared game cards for Religious Smarts (see Preparation)

• *(optional)* screen, computer, and LCD projector for panel discussion

Preparation:

1. Determine how many groups of three or four you will have for small group discussions. Choose that many of the Gandhi quotes interspersed throughout the text or from Appendix C, Quotable Quotes (p. 169), and make three or four copies of each quote. This can be done on colored 3"x 5" note cards, with a different color for each quote so that groups find themselves quickly.

2. For accompaniment for two of the suggested hymns, go to *http://www.hymnsite.com/lyrics/umh582.sht* for "Whom Shall I Send?" *The United Methodist Hymnal*, #582, and to *http://wotruth.com/MIDI/strytotell.mid* for "We've a Story to Tell to the Nations," *The United Methodist Hymnal*, #560.

3. Plan to sing "Saranam, Saranam" (*The United Methodist Hymnal*, #523).

4. For the Religious Smarts activity (Appendix F, option 1, p. 176) photocopy and cut apart the game cards, one set for each small group. If you use option 2, you'll need the list of statements for the moderator to randomly read.

5. Print the following on the chalk or dry erase board or on a sheet of newsprint: Christianity, Islam, Buddhism, Jainism, Hinduism, Sikhism.

6. Obtain a copy of the video or DVD of *Gandhi—the Salt March* and a TV and VCR or DVD player. If you have the video, cue it up to the appropriate place for the activity. Check the activity below to see the appropriate times for the segment on DVD.

7. If you are comfortable using PowerPoint, you could have the readers for the panel presentation sit behind a screen where you can show images of the real speakers and maps found at the following site: *http://news.bbc.co.uk/1/shared/spl/hi/south_asia/02/voices_from_kashmir/html/default.stm*.

8. Prepare an action board by printing the following question on a sheet of newsprint or poster board: "What might I do in response to this study?"

Gandhi Quotes:

As participants enter the classroom, give each person a Gandhi quote. Have class members find others who have the same quote. This will determine the composition of the small groups for this session.

Opening Worship (20 minutes):

Bible Study and Reflection:

Have a volunteer read John 20:19-29. Then read the following, or put it in your own words:

> Each of the gospels and the book of Acts contain a variation of the Great Commission—the sending of the apostles into all the world to spread the good news (Matthew 28:16-20; Mark 16:14-18; Luke 24:36-49; Acts 1:6-8). What a poignant episode we find in the book of John—Thomas is absent when the others receive this assignment. The doubts of Thomas are allayed by Jesus a week later. Tradition has it that Thomas traveled to India to spread the good news there. At the St. Thomas Day celebration in New Delhi on December 18, 1955, Dr. Rajendra Prasad, the first President of India, said: "St. Thomas came to India when many of the countries of Europe had not yet become Christian, and so those Indians who trace their Christianity to him have a longer history and a higher ancestry than that of Christians of many of the European countries." Tradition also tells us that Thomas was martyred in India.

In small groups, discuss the following:

– Name a time you shared your faith with another person. Was this difficult?

– What were some of the dynamics of "successfully" sharing your faith with others?

– What do you think would be some of the challenges if you were a member of a minority religion within a country?

– How might you witness if you were not allowed to preach?

Hymn Singing:

Sing "Saranam, Saranam" (*The United Methodist Hymnal*, #523). If you like, also sing one of the following hymns:

• "Whom Shall I Send?" *The United Methodist Hymnal*, #582 (for accompaniment, go to *http://www.hymnsite.com/lyrics/umh582.sht*;

• "Help Us Accept Each Other," *The United Methodist Hymnal*, #569;

• "We've a Story to Tell to the Nations," *The United Methodist Hymnal*, #560 (for accompaniment, go to *http://wotruth.com/MIDI/strytotell.mid*.

Prayer:

Pray the following, or have participants pray in unison:

O God, give us a vision for mission, as you gave to Thomas and the other disciples. May we dream of the needs of others, and how your church can help them. Heal us of divisions and strife. If there is conflict, make it creative tension rather than divisive argument and fruitless pettiness. Make us aware of those whose hearts are open to the leading of your Spirit. Move us to meet them, listen to their yearnings, and respond to their hopes and dreams. May we not be so rigid that our ears are closed to new ideas and opportunities. In Jesus' name we pray. Amen.

Clorinda's Story (5 minutes):

Ask the person who volunteered to read this story of love played out in the context of colonial mission (p. 42). Then discuss the following:

– After hearing this account, what do you know about Indian society and the role of women during colonial times? (e.g., Brahmin caste, child marriage, practice of sati.)

Religious Sensitivities (10 minutes):

Introduce this exercise by giving participants the following information:

In chapters 2 and 3, Dr. Dhamaraj gave us an outline of the religious history of India and Pakistan, and a sense of the importance of religion in determining a country's destiny. Although the majority of people in India are Hindu, India also contains a rich diversity of religions. Pakistan, on the other hand, was a nation created to accommodate a majority Muslim population, the second largest Muslim population in the world. Even though other religions may claim only a small percentage of the total population in India and Pakistan, that percentage of over a billion people turns out to be a rather large number. Approximately 3 percent of the entire population of India and Pakistan are Christian. There are about 30 million Christians living in India and 2,800,000 living in Pakistan.

Tell participants that in *Creating Interfaith Community*, R. Marston Speight says that interfaith community offers us the possibility of reaching out to those of other faiths and seeking community with them. Essential elements of that community are: (1) that participants act and relate to one another because of their faith, and (2) that they retain their own religious beliefs and practices without giving up any of their religion's distinctiveness. The religious groups in India and Pakistan have had a long history of meeting the challenge of developing relationships within their countries and across borders with people of other faiths. As the majority religion in the United States, we Christians live in a much richer interfaith environment than that of the past. We need to make the most of the opportunity to be in dialogue with those believers so that we can work with them within our communities and develop relationships with them.

Ask participants to turn to "Quotations from Holy Books" (Appendix H, p. 183). Have them work together in their small groups to find the source of each quote. Go over the answers and survey the groups to see how they did. Debrief by asking:

  – What commonalities do you see between six of the religions found in India and Pakistan?

Religious Smarts (15 minutes):
Invite participants to play the game found in Class Tasks, Appendix I (p. 184). If you have a copy of *Creating Interfaith Community*, have it available as a reference.

The Colonial Period and Gandhi (10 minutes):
Read the following background information (or put it in your own words):

Four centuries of European intervention in Indian affairs brought serious negative consequences. The British disrupted the industry and trade of India, making changes to benefit themselves. In the midst of immense ethnic, linguistic, and religious diversity, colonialism brought certain benefits: a nationwide railway system, a second language (English) that could be spoken across the country, and a civil service. Nevertheless, power and profit determined governing decisions and rulers were often insensitive to the culture and the needs of the people. Dr. Dharmaraj writes of how the Enfield rifle, cotton, and salt were important elements in mobilizing the Indian people to revolt against British rule.

In the midst of the Indian battle against injustice, and for freedom, arose one of the most Christ-like figures in Indian history. Mohandas Gandhi, a Hindu, advocated non-violent civil disobedience to combat injustice. The way Gandhi lived his life and the methods he urged to bring about the downfall of British rule reflected the teachings of the Christ.

E. Stanley Jones, named "Missionary Extraordinary" by the Methodist missionary publication *World Outlook* in 1959, wrote a fascinating account of this man shortly after his death. In *Gandhi: Portrayal of a Friend*, Jones recounts that as a young man Gandhi attended Christian church services during his years in South Africa. Gandhi struggled over whether or not he should become a Christian. He shared two observations with E. Stanley Jones. The first was that the sermons were very boring. The second was that the Christians he observed were not acting like Christ.

Have participants discuss the following:

  – What does this say to us about the responsibility of those called to preach? *(Note: Don't allow this to become a bash the preacher session. We are not to judge others, but this question becomes a powerful challenge to reflect upon for those called to preach.)*

– What does this say to those of us who have committed our lives to the Christ (the most powerful message we communicate happens before we ever speak a word)?

– In the past week were there times when your actions did not match what you say you believe?

Video Clip (35 minutes):

Show a clip of the video/DVD *Gandhi—the Salt March.* If you are using the DVD, begin at 2:01:30 and end at 2:20:40. If you are using the video, start when Gandhi begins the march and end as the viceroy requests his attendance at an all-government conference in London. Ask the small groups to be listening for the following as they watch the clip:

– What was it like to be an Indian under British rule?

– Why did Gandhi choose the issue of salt to make a stand?

– What can you glean about Gandhi's rules for passive resistance against injustice?

– On his march to the sea, Gandhi says that it is not the British who are in control, but rather he is. What does he mean by this?

– What movement in the United States parallels Gandhi's use of non-violent civil disobedience and his eventual assassination? (Martin Luther King, Jr.'s civil disobedience and the civil rights movement.)

Voices from Kashmir (20 minutes):

Explain to the participants that some special guests have flown in from the Kashmir region of India. They have agreed to share their stories so that we might better understand the complex human situation that exists in Kashmir.

• Arrange four chairs at the front of the classroom—one for yourself (or a volunteer) as moderator, and three for the participants who agreed to take the parts of the "special guests." Introduce each guest with the background information at the beginning of this section.

• If you are using PowerPoint as suggested in the Preparation, set up panel members' chairs behind the screen.

Tell participants to listen for:

• words of hope and words of despair;

• an explanation of the cause;

• words that might describe life in Kashmir.

When the panel presentation is concluded, ask participants to discuss the following in their small groups:

– Does each person's age, family circumstance, religion, education, and so forth make life any easier or more difficult?

– What is the role of the governments of India and Pakistan?

– How might the church or individual Christians impact the situation in Kashmir (Track happenings in the news; write to congressmen/women; etc.).

Brainstorm (5 minutes):

Call participants' attention to the question on the action board you prepared: "What might I do in response to this study?" Have them brainstorm suggestions and print them on the board (organize the India/Pakistan study for your unit or church school class, and so forth).

Closing Responsive Prayer (5 minutes):

Designate the right and left side of the class and pray the following responsive prayer together:

R: O Lord, we are grateful for missionaries…

L: Who answer your call to serve in our land and far away.

R: We give you praise for those Christians who are the minority religion.

L: And still are willing to commit their lives to you and witness to your presence in their lives.

R: We thank you for inspiring people like Gandhi and all those who work for peace;

L: To lead others to fight injustice.

R: Be with those who live in Kashmir.

L: Help them to be faithful to your presence.

R: Be with those in positions of power.

L: Help them to work for justice and peace.

All: **Give us a willingness to serve you and a commitment to work for peace with justice in your world. In Jesus' name we pray. Amen.**

Assignments:

• Ask participants to read chapters 4 and 5.

• Remind participants to work on their class tasks for session 4.

• Ask for two volunteers to read/act out a short conversation between Isabella Thoburn and Clara Swain (Appendix J, p. 186), and a volunteer to learn and sing the benediction song "God of Creation," (*Global Praise I*, #8), and "Jaya Ho" (*The United Methodist Hymnal*, #478).

Session

3

Objectives:

1. To appreciate and support with prayer the institutions (hospitals and schools) begun and run by the church in India and Pakistan.

2. To explore the varied benefits of the Jamkhed Comprehensive Rural Health Program.

3. To gain an understanding of the status of women in India.

Materials and Supplies:

• slips of paper with one of the institutions or ministries named in chapter 4

• 3" x 5" note cards cut in half (white and two colors, or just white with three colors of fine-lined felt-tipped markers)

• adding machine tape (or long strips of paper for timeline)

• *Prayer Calendar*, *Catalog of General Advance Projects* and *Global Praise I*.

• copy of video, *Healing the Whole Person*, and a

TV/VCR

• several pieces of cloth or scarves

• copies of *The United Methodist Hymnal*

Preparation:

1. Prepare a slip of paper for each participant with one of the following institutions or ministries named in chapter 4: Isabella Thoburn College, India; Kinnaird College for Women in Pakistan; Lucy Harrison Girls' High School, Lahore, Pakistan; Calcutta Girls' High School, India; Sarah Tucker College for Women; Clara Swain Hospital; Vellore Christian College and Hospital; Comprehensive Rural Health Program, Jamkhed, India; The United Christian Hospital, Pakistan.

2. Get some lengths of cloth or scarves to use in the opening worship.

3. Cut three strips of paper from a roll of adding machine tape, and fasten them parallel to each

other along a wall or on a bulletin board. Label the first strip "Indian/Pakistani Time Line," the second "World Time Line," and the last "United States Time Line."

4. Cut 3" x 5" note cards in half (using a combination of white and two other colors of cards, or just white cards with three colors of fine-point, felt-tipped markers).

5. Using information from chapter 4 (and whatever other sources are helpful), prepare a short presentation about the status of women today in India and Pakistan. Include information on some or all of the following: the education of a girl child, women's invisible work, honor killings, the Hadood Ordinances, dowry and bride price, and stove-burning.

6. For the simulation, the introduction included in the activity could be taped and played to the class (similar to the beginning of the old "Mission Impossible" TV program. Go to *http://www.discoverynet.com/~ajsnead/allsongs_1/mission2.html* for music to set the stage.

7. Obtain a copy of the video, *Healing the Whole Person*, and a TV/VCR. Select a short segment to show, or use the suggested segment. Also print the questions included in the activity on a chalk or dry erase board or a sheet of newsprint. Cover the questions with a blank sheet of newsprint until you're ready for the class to view them.

8. You will also need a copy of the *Prayer Calendar* and the *Catalog of General Advance Projects* and *Global Praise I*.

9. Go over the hymn, "Jaya Ho" (*The United Methodist Hymnal*, #478). Ask a pianist to be prepared to play the hymn for the group.

Mission Projects in India/Pakistan (5 minutes):

As participants enter the classroom, give them one of the slips of paper you prepared with the name of one of the institutions or ministries the church supports in India (found in chapter 4). Ask class members to find others with the same mission project to determine their discussion groups.

– Have participants scan through chapter 4 to learn about their projects. Suggest that the institution named on their slip might become their prayer project for the remainder of the time in this study, and longer if they are willing.

– Ask participants to identify the problems that their project is working to alleviate.

Opening Worship (10 minutes):

Bible Study and Reflection:

Ask a volunteer to read Luke 13:10-13. Then ask:

– What are the things that "bend-over" the women (people) of India and Pakistan (the problems the discussion groups have been identifying: poverty, no health care, illiteracy, the traditions concerning Dalits, dowry, widow burning)?

Have the volunteer stand up and bend over at the waist. With each affliction named, place a scarf or piece of cloth on the volunteer's back.

Guide the discussion toward an understanding that if any of God's people are experiencing injustice and are not able to use their God-given gifts, all of society suffers. Ask the following:

– What institutions or ministries supported by The United Methodist Church take away the burdens of the bent-over people of India and Pakistan?

With each ministry or institution named, remove one of the scarves and ask the volunteer to stand a little straighter.

Hymn Singing:

Ask the volunteer who learned "Jaya Ho" (*The United Methodist Hymnal*, #478) to sing it through once. Then sing the hymn together.

Prayer:

Pray the following:

Lord, we offer to you our silent prayers for the work being done in your name in India and Pakistan (*allow a moment of silence*). **Amen.**

Historical Time Line Overview (10 minutes):

Divide the class into six groups. Groups 1-4 get white cards. Groups 5 and 6 get note cards of two different colors (alternative: use white note cards and three different colored fine-point, felt-tipped markers). Assign the following tasks to the group to complete, using Appendix D, Time Lines (p. 172). Have the participants working on the India/Pakistan Time Line place their information first so that those working on the World and the United States Time Lines can place their information in parallel lines at the appropriate dates.

Group 1: Choose four events from Indian history prior to the time of Christ. Print the date and a descriptive phrase on one of the four white cards, then attach the cards to the first quarter of the Indian/Pakistani Time Line with double-sided tape.

Group 2: Choose four events from Indian history between the time of Christ and 1900. Print the date and a descriptive phrase on one of the four cards, then attach the cards to the second quarter of the Indian/Pakistani Time Line with double-sided tape.

Group 3: Choose four events from Indian history between 1900 and 1947. Print the date and a descriptive phrase on one of the four cards, then attach the cards to the third quarter of the Indian/Pakistani Time Line with double-sided tape.

Group 4: Choose four events from Indian history between 1948 and the present. Print the date and a descriptive phrase on one of the four cards, then attach the cards to the fourth quarter of the Indian/Pakistani Time Line with double-sided tape.

Group 5: Chose eight events from world history (four prior to the time of Christ, four after the time of Christ). Print the date and a descriptive phrase on one of the colored cards, then attach the cards to the World Time Line with double-sided tape.

Group 6: Choose six events from U.S. history. Print the date and a descriptive phrase on one of the colored cards, then attach the cards to the United States Time Line with double-sided tape.

Conversation between Clara Swain and Isabelle Thoburn (10 minutes):

Introduce this dialogue by telling participants that two special guests are visiting the class today. Then have the participants who volunteered to take the parts of Clara Swain and Isabella Thoburn read the dialogue. Discuss the following:

- What were some of the special challenges for missionary women?

Study Leader Presentation (20 minutes):

Using information from chapter 4 (and whatever other sources are helpful), give some highlights about the status of women today in India and Pakistan. You might include information on the education of a girl child and women's invisible work, as well as about honor killings, the Hadood Ordinances, dowry and bride price, and stove-burning.

Jamkhed Simulation—Mission Possible (20 minutes):

Each discussion group will act as a team (or if you have a small class, have everybody tackle this together). Have each group put their results on a piece of newsprint. If you prepared a taped introduction, play it, or just have the class hum for about fifteen seconds, then turn down the volume and read the following script:

> Your mission, Christians, should you choose to accept it, will take you halfway around the world. You will be sent to an extremely poor area in the Indian state of Maharashtra. Your constituency will include 250 villages, encompassing 250,000 people. You will have to treat people with leprosy, tuberculosis, malnutrition, and diarrhea; a population with a high birth rate and a high infant mortality rate. The situation is one of extreme poverty. Two doctors (a married couple) will help you fulfill this mission. You will begin with no funding, no facilities, and no equipment. You must put together an action plan for comprehensive community-based primary health care. To do this you must determine what makes a program comprehensive; what makes it community-based; and what makes it primary health care. Determine what your guiding principles will be as you work on your assignment. How will you tackle this mission? This tape will self-destruct in thirty seconds!

Ask the small groups to come up with a plan of action to address this mission. When groups have had a few minutes to work, have a representative from each group share the results of their "consultation" with the rest of the class.

Ask the following:

- What do you know about health care in your own community?

- Who has access?

- What groups of people are shut out from comprehensive health care in the U. S.?

- What kinds of actions are called for to make health care comprehensive in our own country?

View Video Clip (5 minutes):

View a short clip from the video *Healing the Whole Person*. One suggested portion is a four-minute clip from time code 00:50-4:55.

The Real Results (5 minutes):

Ask participants to respond to the following:

- What parallels did you find between the Jamkhed project and your action plans?

Uncover the following information from the video

study guide you prepared in advance:

- Relying on the whole community and the richness of its resources, the Drs. Arole have created a preventative medical practice.

- Infant mortality has been reduced by two-thirds.

- Malnutrition has been reduced from 60 percent to 3 percent.

- Diarrhea rarely kills anymore.

- New incidents of leprosy are almost nonexistent.

- Tuberculosis is in check.

- Comprehensive community-based primary health care has now been successfully introduced into eighteen project sites in twelve countries, with each project being tailored to the culture and natural resources of the individual communities.

Mission Outreach (20 minutes):

Remind participants that United Methodist Women support mission projects around the world with their Undesignated Giving. Read the following, or give the information in your own words:

Undesignated Giving—close to $20 million a year—provides food, shelter, education, employment, health care, and human rights advocacy for those most oppressed and forgotten. Money is distributed annually through an appropriations process by the elected directors of the Women's Division. Through their channels, United Methodist Women also support mission projects that impact women, children, and youth.

A congregation's first call to mission is to make sure it pays its World Service apportionment and conference benevolence. The World Service Fund undergirds all mission programs of The United Methodist Church, including the Advance. The Advance is an official, second-mile channel for designated giving in The United Methodist Church. The Advance is called designated giving because it is a way for individuals, church groups, congregations, districts, and annual conferences to select specific ministries to support voluntarily. For more than fifty years, United Methodists have given more than three million Advance gifts totaling nearly $900 million for thousands of ministries in more than one hundred countries. The actual amount of Advance funding that a project receives is solely dependent upon donor response. A unique feature of the Advance is that 100 percent of every donation to a General Advance project will go to that project (administrative and promotional expenses are paid by other sources of funds).

Ask participants to choose a project to support for the coming year with prayer. They can use the following resources for possible projects:

- *Prayer Calendar*
- the mission maps on the UMW website
  (http://gbgm-umc.org/umw/umwmap/Mapug/Mapmain.htm#)
- the *Catalog of General Advance Projects*
- *http://www.umcgiving.org/content/offsite.asp?url=http:// gbgm-umc.org/advproj* (The Advance website)

Ask participants to share information about projects with their small groups.

Brainstorm (5 minutes):

Call participants' attention to the action board from session 2 with the question, "What might I do in response to this study?" Have them brainstorm additional suggestions in the light of this session's activities and print them on the board (provide monetary support for a project in India/Pakistan; do a program for my unit on the Jamkhed project; keep my project in prayer for a year; send birthday cards to missionaries in India/Pakistan).

Benediction Song (5 minutes):

Close with "God of Creation," *Global Praise I*, #8 sung by a volunteer, or have the class read the song as a prayer benediction.

Assignment:

• participants to read chapters 6 and 7, paying particular attention to the description of the seven Indian theologies (Dalit Theology; Indian Liberation Theology; Theology of Religious Pluralism; Post-Colonial Theology; Women's Theology; Indigenous Theology; Harmony Theology). Tell them a portion of class discussion will ask them to identify the theology that most closely matches their own theology.

• Remind class members that they will be sharing whatever they have prepared (Class Tasks) for the "India/Pakistan TV Special."

Session

4

Objectives:

1. To investigate the differences between Western and Indian theologies;

2. To learn more about the variety of Christian theologies that exist in India;

3. To examine the problem of working children, focusing on rug makers in Pakistan;

4. To commit to take some form of action in response to what's been experienced in this study.

Materials and Supplies:

- Videos: *When Children Do the Work* and *One Child's Labor*

- TV, VCR

- votive candles for each class member, white Christ candle, and matches

- symbols used throughout the study for the worship center table

- copies of *Global Praise 1*

- *(optional)* copies of *The Faith We Sing*

- copies of *The United Methodist Hymnal*

- Bibles

- 3" x 5" note cards and pencils for each participant

- newsprint, chalkboard, or dry erase board with printed definitions of theologies of the subcontinent (see Preparation)

- dry erase board and markers, chalkboard and chalk, or newsprint; two colors of markers; tape

Preparation:

Obtain copies of the suggested videos and a TV and VCR. Cue up each tape to the suggested segments.

For the discussion of theologies of the subcontinent, print definitions of theologies (the material within the brackets) on a dry erase board, chalkboard, or a sheet of newsprint.

Gather the supplies and materials you need for the Service of Commitment. If you have access to *The Faith We Sing* hymnbook, "The Summons" has powerful words and is very singable (alternate option: "Here I Am, Lord," *The United Methodist Hymnal*, #593).

On-The-Spot Survey (5 minutes):

Do a quick survey of the participants by asking the following questions:

– When did you get your first job?

– When did you start earning a living and support yourself or your family?

Hymn Singing (5 minutes):

Sing "Saranam, Saranam" (*The United Methodist Hymnal*, #523) and "Jaya Ho" (*The United Methodist Hymnal*, #478).

Video Viewing (30 minutes):

Show a twelve minute segment of the video, *When Children Do the Work*, in which twelve-year-old Iqbal Masih stands up for his rights and the rights of other rug makers in Pakistan, and is murdered for his efforts. Ask participants to brainstorm ways that we might make a difference in this situation. Put ideas on newsprint or the chalkboard or dry erase board.

Next view the thirteen minute segment of the video, *One Child's Labor*, from the TV News Magazine, *60 Minutes*. After reading about Iqbal Masih's murder, thirteen-year-old Canadian Craig Kielburger mobilized himself and other young people to address the problem of child labor. Compare what Craig and other children have done with the list developed by the class. Add to the list using another color marker.

Special Simulated Documentary on India and Pakistan (50-60 minutes):

Have participants share what they've prepared from Appendix I, "Documentary Special on India & Pakistan: Class Tasks" (p. 184). After each presentation, allow a few minutes for questions or comments.

Indian Theology: Small Group Discussions (30 minutes):

Say the following, or put it in your own words:

In the 2003 mission study *Creating Interfaith Community*, there were many opportunities to learn about other faiths, their mission and beliefs, and how these faiths live in U.S. society. In chapter 5 of this study on India and Pakistan, Jacob Dharmaraj opens up to new forms of theology on the subcontinent which are helping people live in an interfaith context.

Ask participants to discuss the following:

– How do you respond to the various approaches of Indian and Pakistani Christians to living as Christians in modern society on the subcontinent? What does this say to you about how you live in modern U.S. society?

– Many forms of modern U.S. Christian theology have arisen to counter bigotry and oppression. Name some of these theologies (Feminist, Womanist, Black or African-American, Hispanic theologies) which were the result of the impact of Liberation Theology. What impact have these theologies had on your thinking and faith? What impact do you think they have on Indian and Pakistani Christians?

Service of Commitment (20 minutes):

Give a 3" x 5" note card and a pencil to each participant. Along with other symbols on the worship center table, add a votive candle for each participant and a large white Christ candle and matches.

Scripture:

Ask a volunteer to read the scripture, Luke 10:1-9.

Hymn:

Sing "The Summons" *(The Faith We Sing)* or "Here I Am, Lord," *The United Methodist Hymnal*, #593).

Affirmation of Faith:

Use *"An Affirmation of Faith: The Common Mat of God's Grace"* by Glory Dharmaraj (p. 6).

Reflection:

Read the following, or put it in your own words:

When Jesus sent out the seventy-two, they were to travel lightly, accept whatever hospitality was given, heal the sick, and spread the good news that "the Kingdom of God has come near to you." How many times do we become prisoners of our suitcases? How many times do we complain about the food or the accommodations that are offered to us? How many times have we neglected to do what we can do?

"In a huge conference hall in Washington, D.C., over a thousand participants listen with rapt attention to Muktabai Pol, a village health worker from Jamkhed, India…. Muktabai shares her experience of providing primary health care in a remote Indian village. She concludes her speech by pointing to the glittering lights in the hall. 'This is a beautiful hall and the shining chandeliers are a treat to watch,' she says. 'One has to travel thousands of miles to come to see their beauty. The doctors are like these chandeliers, beautiful and exquisite, but expensive and inaccessible.' She then pulls out two wick lamps from her purse. She lights one. 'This lamp is inexpensive and simple, but unlike the chandeliers, it can transfer its light to another lamp.' She lights the other wick lamp with the first. Holding up both lamps in her outstretched hands she says, 'I am like this lamp, lighting the lamp of better health. Workers like me can light another and another and thus encircle the whole earth. This is Health for All.'" (From *Jamkhed: A Comprehensive Rural Health Project*, by Doctors Mabelle and Rajanikant Arole.)

Act of Commitment:

Say the following:

Sometimes we are the ones called to go and serve; sometimes we are the ones called to enable others to serve. What are you being called to do in response to this class?

Have a volunteer quietly sing the hymn, "The Summons," and allow people to write on their cards what they will do in the following year in response to this course. Have class members bring their note cards to the altar table and light a votive candle as they silently pray for their "projects," and as a symbol of their commitment to respond to the Spirit's call.

Closing Prayer:

Close with a prayer of your own, or with prayer and "God of Creation (Benediction)," *Global Praise I*, #8).

APPENDICES

APPENDIX A
INDIAN AND PAKISTANI RECIPES

As there are over a billion people in India and Pakistan and the countries include many cultures, climates, and customs, so there are thousands of dishes and attempts to please every taste. There are also many variations on recipes for the same dish. In one Indian cooking class, participants were encouraged not to worry if they couldn't find an ingredient. The teacher suggested we become familiar with Indian cooking and substitute other ingredients. She urged us to adjust the mixture of spices to individual preferences for hot or mild.

Staple Foods of India

In the north, wheat is made into bread. Examples of common Indian breads are Roti, Chappati, Puri, Naan, and Paratha. Indian breads are very different from the traditional western bread. In northern and central India, people usually serve their meal with Roti, which is a flat bread and resembles a tortilla. Roti are usually unleavened (made without yeast or any other leavening agent). Indian breads are usually made from whole wheat flour. Naan is a flat bread made with yeast. In the south, rice is a staple.

Most Indian/Pakistani cooks have their own favorite recipes for "curry," and they vary according to the dishes being cooked. If you go into an Indian/Pakistani grocery store (and many large grocery stores) here in the United States, you will find curry powders, a mixture of spices for the convenience of cooking in the United States. Curry powders vary greatly in strength and taste. Generally the Indian/Pakistani powders and pastes are hotter, but you can find mild mixtures. All curries contain the same six basic ingredients: coriander, turmeric, cumin seed, fenugreek, black pepper, and cayenne or chili pepper. After these six, there are at least twenty other ingredients that might be included in a curry.

Curried Cabbage

Most Hindu people are vegetarian. The following is a vegetarian recipe that uses the pre-mixed commercially available curry powder.

½ tsp. thyme	salt and pepper to taste	2 onions, chopped
2 T. curry powder	1 large cabbage, chopped	1 sweet red pepper, chopped
2 c. chicken broth	2 celery stalks, chopped	2 small carrots
¼ tsp. hot pepper flakes		

Bring first four ingredients to a boil. Add chopped cabbage, onions, celery, and red pepper to the stock and herbs. Cut the carrots into julienne strips and add last. Cook until tender on medium-high heat.

Serves four.

Red Lentil Dal

Dal is a spicy dish made with lentils, tomatoes, onions, and various seasonings. Dal is often puréed and served with curried dishes. In India, the term "dal" refers to any of almost sixty varieties of dried legumes, including peas, mung beans, and lentils. This traditional Indian dish is usually served with basmati rice or Indian bread.

1 T. vegetable oil	½ tsp. ground cumin
2 c. chopped onions	½ tsp. ground ginger
2 garlic cloves, minced	1 c. basmati rice,* cooked according to package directions
3 c. water	2 plum tomatoes, seeded and chopped
1 c. dried red lentils*	¼ c. chopped fresh cilantro
½ tsp. turmeric	1 jalapeño chili pepper, seeded and chopped

Available at Indian markets and in many supermarkets

Heat oil in medium skillet over medium-high heat. Add 1 cup onion and 1 minced garlic clove and sauté until tender and golden brown, about 10 minutes. Set aside. Combine 3 cups water, lentils, remaining 1 cup onion, 1 minced garlic clove, turmeric, cumin, and ginger in heavy medium saucepan. Bring to boil. Reduce heat, cover, and simmer until lentils are tender, about 15 minutes. Transfer half of lentil mixture to a food processor and purée until smooth. Return purée to same saucepan. Mix in sautéed onion mixture. Simmer 5 minutes to blend flavors. Season to taste with salt and pepper. Spoon rice into bowls and top with the dal. Garnish with tomatoes, cilantro, and chili.

Serves four.

Per serving: calories, 410; total fat, 5 g; saturated fat, 1 g; cholesterol, 0 mg.

(Adapted from *Bon Appétit*, March 1999)

Gajar Halva (Sweet Carrot Pudding)

In India Gajar Halva is served warm, mounded in the center of a dish, and garnished with chopped nuts. I tested this dessert dish on senior citizens at a covered dish dinner. They loved it. Because I was in a hurry, I shortened the cooking time a bit. This made the pudding a little thinner than it should have been.

6 carrots (about 1 lb.), scraped and shredded	¼ c. butter, margarine, or ghee
2 c. cream or half-and-half	½ tsp. ground cardamom
½ c. brown sugar	salt to taste
½ c. golden seedless raisins	½ c. slivered almonds (+ slivered almonds to garnish)

Bring carrots and cream to a boil over medium-high heat. Reduce heat to simmer and cook until liquid is almost absorbed (about 1 hour). Add raisins for the last 15 minutes so they can plump. When the liquid is almost absorbed, add brown sugar, butter (or margarine or ghee), cardamom, nuts, and salt. Gently stir and cook the mixture until sugar is dissolved (about 2 minutes).

Serves six to eight.

Sweet Mango Lassi

The New Food Lover's Companion, Second Edition, by Sharon Tyler Herbst gives the following definition for lassi: "A popular chilled yogurt drink in India, which can also be made with buttermilk or extra-rich milk. Lassi is like a healthy milk shake, the thickness of which depends on the ratio of yogurt to water. Thick lassi is made with four parts yogurt to one part water and/or crushed ice. Lassi can be flavored variously with salt, mint, cumin, sugar, fruit, or fruit juices—even spicy additions such as ground chilies, fresh ginger, or garlic. The ingredients are all placed in a blender and processed until the mixture is light and frothy."

Try the following recipe as a treat for your class. The bubbly froth subsides when lassi stands awhile, so whip it again in the blender or whisk it just before serving.

- 3 c. yogurt
- 1 c. mango purée (fresh or canned Indian Alphonso mango purée)
- ½ c. sugar
- 2 c. ice cubes

Put all the ingredients in an electric blender or food processor and blend until the ice is crushed and the liquid is frothy. Serve immediately in tall glasses. The drink will keep, covered, for up to 3 days in the refrigerator. Whip again before serving.

Serves four.

Foods of Pakistan

Although many Indians are vegetarian because of Hindu beliefs, the great majority of Pakistanis are Muslim. They eat meat, but no pork.

Chapli Kebab

These are actually meat patties and not kebabs, which are skewered meat chunks. Ghee is clarified butter. The water and nonfat solids are separated and removed by gently heating and removing with a spoon. Ghee doesn't sputter or burn, has an excellent flavor, and will keep for a long time, even unrefrigerated. During the "Festival of Lights" in India, thousands of clay lamps are fueled with ghee.

1 lb. finely ground beef or lamb	1 green chili pepper or jalapeño, seeded and finely chopped
1 egg	3 to 5 T. ghee or vegetable oil
2 tsp. curry powder	1 onion, thinly sliced for garnish
juice of ½ lemon	1 T. chopped fresh cilantro (coriander) for garnish

Combine well the meat, egg, curry powder, lemon juice, and chili pepper. Divide into 4 oval-shaped patties, each ½ inch thick. Heat ghee or oil in skillet over medium-high heat. Add patties, reduce heat to medium, and fry about eight minutes on each side or until brown (add more oil if necessary). Serve garnished with onion slices and chopped cilantro.

Am Ki Chatni (Fresh Mango and Coconut Chutney)

In Indian cuisine, a chutney is a fruit condiment which contains vinegar, spices, and sometimes nuts. Its texture can range from smooth to chunky and its taste varies from sweet to tart, and from mild to spicy. The most common chutney is mango. Try serving this chutney with your curry dishes.

1 mango (about 1 lb.) peeled, seeded, and cut in small chunks	1 T. finely chopped fresh ginger or 1 tsp. ground ginger
½ c. shredded coconut	½ tsp. salt
¼ c. finely chopped cilantro	½ tsp. dried red pepper flakes

Toss ingredients together and chill. Serve in a separate bowl as a condiment with meat or chicken curries.

Makes about 2 cups.

Fresh Peach Chutney

Indian cooks use the fruits that are available to them. You might want to try this peach chutney when peaches are in season.

1 firm ripe peach	¼ tsp. ground cumin
¼ c. golden raisins, finely chopped	1 T. sugar
1 T. fresh gingerroot, peeled and finely chopped	1 T. fresh orange juice
1½ tsp. shallot, finely chopped	1 tsp. fresh lemon juice
1 fresh serrano or jalapeño chili pepper, seeded and finely chopped (wear rubber gloves)	

Toss ingredients together and chill. Serve in a separate bowl as a condiment with meat or chicken curries.

Makes about 2 cups.

APPENDIX B
CROSSWORD

Across

4. The non-violent "right conduct" of Jainism

8. Hindu greeting, spoken with palms pressed together, which honors the person greeted

11. Creamy yogurt drink

12. Hindu god

13. Organization of monks and nuns in Buddhism

15. Disk-shaped unleavened bread

16. Location of the holiest shrine of Sikhism

18. Caste mark worn by Hindu women on their forehead

19. The Hindu practice of burning the widow

20. Early invaders of India

21. Hindu mystical writings

24. Indian bishop who paved the way for the church of South India

25. Tea

26. Religious and philosophical writings (1000-600 BCE)

27. Male garment, traditional loin wrap

28. Clarified butter

Down

1. The world's largest democracy

2. In the Buddhist and Hindu religions, the force produced by a person's actions in one of their lives which influences what happens to them in their future lives

3. The founder of Sikhism

5. One of the first female missionaries sent to India by the Woman's Foreign Missionary Society in 1869 (two words)

6. A place of spiritual retreat

7. One of the first female missionaries sent to India by the Woman's Foreign Missionary Society in 1869 (two words)

9. Gandhi's autobiography (four words)

10. Epic that contains the Hindu scripture Bhagavad Gita

14. Gandhi's soul force

17. An extremist Hindu movement

22. First president of India

23. Symbol of Gandhi's identification with the poor (two words)

25. Role of social divisions

India Pakistan

Created by Diane Miller with EclipseCrossword *(www.eclipsecrossword.com)*

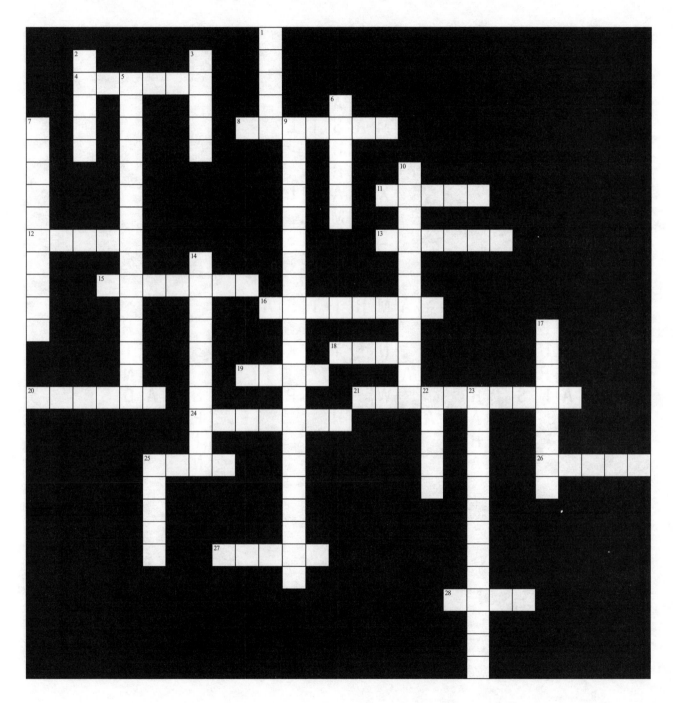

India Pakistan–Answers

Created by Diane Miller with EclipseCrossword *(www.eclipsecrossword.com)*

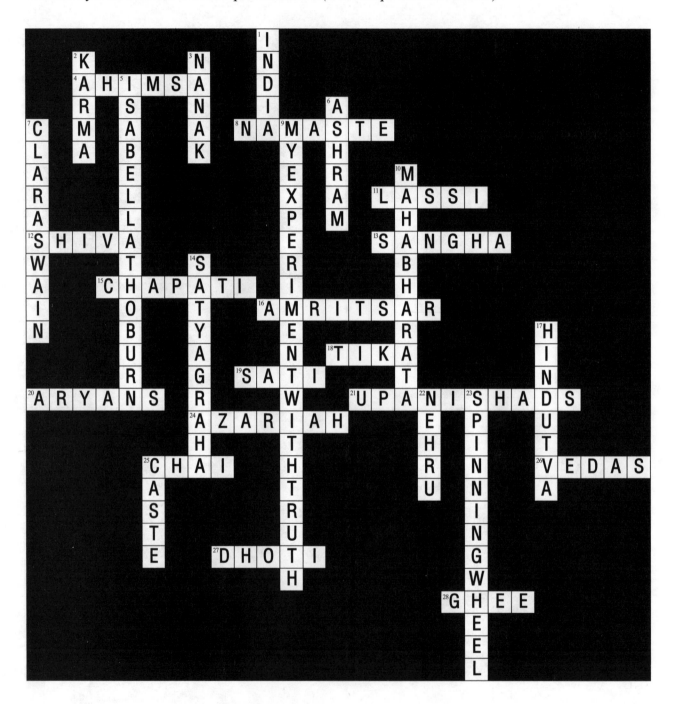

Mohandas K. Gandhi

It is unwise to be too sure of one's own wisdom. It is healthy to be reminded that the strongest might weaken and the wisest might err.

I object to violence because when it appears to do good, the good is only temporary; the evil it does is permanent.

The weak can never forgive. Forgiveness is the attribute of the strong.

An eye for an eye makes the whole world blind.

Victory attained by violence is tantamount to a defeat, for it is momentary.

What is faith if it is not translated into action?

Nonviolence succeeds only when we have a real living faith in God.

My effort should never be to undermine another's faith but to make him a better follower of his own faith.

There are people in the world so hungry that God cannot appear to them except in the form of bread.

Happiness is when what you think, what you say, and what you do are in harmony.

We must become the change we want to see.

Action may not always bring happiness; but there is no happiness without action.

The fragrance always remains on the hand that gives the rose.

Freedom is not worth having if it does not include the freedom to make mistakes.

Non-cooperation and civil disobedience are different but [are] branches of the same tree called Satyagraha (truth-force).

Intolerance, discourtesy, and harshness are taboo in all good society and are surely contrary to the spirit of democracy.

What difference does it make to the dead, the orphans, and the homeless, whether the mad destruction is wrought under the name of totalitarianism or the holy name of liberty or democracy?

Honest differences are often a healthy sign of progress.

In the attitude of silence the soul finds the path in a clearer light, and what is elusive and deceptive resolves itself into crystal clearness. Our life is a long and arduous quest after Truth.

I have noticed that nothing I have never said ever did me any harm.

Dr. Martin Luther King, Jr.

We have flown the air like birds, and swum the sea like fishes, but we have not learned the simple act of walking the earth like brothers. Now let us begin. Now let us re-dedicate ourselves to the long, bitter—but beautiful—struggle for a new world. The choice is ours, and though we might prefer it otherwise, we must choose in this crucial moment in human history.… Let us be those creative dissenters who will call our beloved nation to a higher destiny, to a new plateau of compassion, to a more noble expression of humaneness.… I refuse to accept the view that man is mere flotsam and jetsam in the river of life which surrounds him. I refuse to accept the view that mankind is so tragically bound to the star-less midnight of racism and war that the bright daylight of peace and brotherhood can never become a reality. I believe that even amid today's mortar bursts and whining bullets, there is still hope for a brighter tomorrow.

—December, 1964, acceptance speech for the Nobel Peace Prize

The ultimate weakness of violence is that it is a descending spiral, begetting the very thing it seeks to destroy. Instead of diminishing evil, it multiplies it.... Through violence you may murder the hater, but you do not murder hate. In fact, violence merely increases hate.... Returning violence for violence multiplies violence, adding deeper darkness to a night already devoid of stars. Darkness cannot drive out hate; only love can do that.

True compassion is more than flinging a coin at a beggar; it comes to see that an edifice which produces beggars needs restructuring.

Love is the only force capable of turning an enemy into a friend.

Other Quotes

The mere threat of trade sanctions led employers in the garment industry of an Asian country to dismiss tens of thousands of children... [who then] shifted into other occupations, which were often more hazardous.

—*The International Labor Organization*

Never doubt that a small group of thoughtful, committed citizens can change the world; indeed, it's the only thing that ever has.

—*Margaret Mead*

The best way to destroy an enemy is to make him a friend.

—*Abraham Lincoln*

Peace starts with a smile.

—*Mother Teresa*

Hold fast to dreams
For when dreams die
Life is a broken-winged bird
That cannot fly.

—*Langston Hughes*

APPENDIX D
TIME LINES

INDIA

2500 BCE	First nation inhabitants in India
2000–600 BCE	Aryan Period
1500–500 BCE	Hindu mystical writings called Upanishads
1000–600 BCE	Vedic Age
563 BCE	Birth of Buddha
540–468 BCE	Founding of Jainism

*****

52 CE	Arrival of Thomas in India
345 CE	Chaldean Christians escape persecution and arrive in India
1498	Vasco da Gama arrives and establishes trade between Portugal and India
1631–1653	Taj Mahal built in India

WORLD

2613–2494 BCE	Egyptian Pyramids
2000 BCE	Abraham, Sarah, and Hagar lived out lives of faith and struggle
1260 BCE	Moses led Hebrew people out of Egypt
1200–323 BCE	Classic Greek culture (Alexander the Great dies in 323 BCE)
753 BCE–476 CE	Roman Empire
587–586 BCE	Fall of Jerusalem to Babylon

*****

475–1453 CE	Middle Ages and Feudalism
622 CE	Muhammad marches from Mecca to Medina; beginning of Muslim era
1500	Height of the Rennaisance
1760–1851	Industrial Revolution in England
1521	Protestant Reformation
1914–1918	World War I

1917	Russian Revolution
1939–1945	World War II
1957	European Free Trade Zone established between six countries
1993	Maastricht Treaty unites Europe
1999	Euro becomes common currency of EEC; USSR and Eastern Block Countries abandon Socialist system

UNITED STATES

1492 CE	Columbus arrives in what is later called the Americas
July 4, 1776	Thirteen English colonies declare independence
1861–1865	American Civil War
1882	U.S. bans Chinese immigration for ten years; Chinese Exclusion Act bans immigration of Chinese laborers to U.S. (repealed in 1943)
1905–1914	Almost 10.5 million immigrants enter U.S. from southern and eastern Europe; Asiatic Exclusion League founded in San Francisco to prevent immigration of Asians; most member organizations are labor unions
1907	Immigration to U.S. restricted by law
1914–1918	World War I
1924–1930	Immigration Quota Act excludes all aliens ineligible for citizenship (all Asians except Hawaiians and Filipinos) and entry of alien wives of Chinese merchants, but not alien wives of U.S. citizens until 1930, when Public Law 349 admits wives married by May 26, 1924
1939–1945	World War II
1945	United Nations organization formed
1950–1953	Korean War
1965	Immigration and Naturalization Act abolishes national quotas and substitutes hemispheric quotas
1969	Americans land on Moon
2001	Patriot Act I passed
2003	Patriot Act II passed

APPENDIX E
FOR THE FUN OF IT

The following are additional activities to enrich the study:

1. Cook some Pakistani food:

http://www.desicookbook.com/. You may not recognize many of the ingredients, but they'll have an active link. Click on the link and discover a picture and another name for the ingredient.

2. Learn to wrap a sari:

http://www.kerala.com/fashion/hwsari.htm.

3. Have an Indian/Pakistani woman demonstrate the use of henna, body art that is not permanent:

http://www.hennapage.com/henna/index.html.

4. Create flower garlands:

Using real flowers: *http://www.save-on-crafts.com/tecformakgar.html*
Using tissue paper flowers: *http://www.azcentral.com/home/crafty/articles/0913craftyideas13.html.*

5. Create candles or small diva lamps:

For directions for making small clay lamps, see the children's study for 2003, *Seven Friends, Seven Faiths.*

6. Write names in Sanskrit:

Have someone from India write each person's first name on a 4" x 6" note card in Sanskrit script. Class members can practice "writing" their name in Sanskrit.

7. Crossword Puzzle:

Have participants work the Crossword Puzzle in Appendix B (p. 166).

8. "Monsoon" Simulation:

Try this simulation with your class. Allow at least two hours. Complete instructions: *http://www.tear.org.au/resources/simgame_monsoon/monsoon.pdf.*

9. Language Map Exercise:

Use the Internet MLA's (Modern Language Association) Language Data Center to learn how many speakers of Hindi (the national language and primary tongue spoken by 30 percent of Indians) there are in the county where you live. [Punjabi (the national language and primary tongue spoken by 48 percent of Pakistanis) would be included under the category "other indic languages."]

• *Go to http://www.mla.org/census_data.*

• Choose "county" under "select type," enter your "state," and click "show result."

• Enter your "county" and click "show result."

APPENDIX F
RELIGIOUS SMARTS

Use the following text to give class participants background information about six religions of India and Pakistan.

Option #1: Using the statements below, cut the sentences into separate strips and have teams try to pair up five statements with the religion they describe.

Option #2: Play a game of "Who Wants To Have Religious Smarts?" (based on "Who Wants to Be a Millionaire?"). Split the class in half and ask the questions in random order. Or have two volunteers compete. Each contestant may call upon someone from the class for help with one answer and may poll the class for help with one answer. Have a scorekeeper keep track of correct answers.

Christianity

Francis Xavier came to the Portuguese possession of Goa in India and converted many to this faith.

Bartholomaeus Ziegenbalg, sent by the Dutch, was the first of this group to come to India in 1706.

Clorinda converted from Hinduism to this religion in the 18th century.

Until 1812, missionaries of this religion were not allowed to stay in the British India Company's colonies or settlements.

Approximately 3% of India's population are followers of this religion.

Islam

The officers connected with the East India Company ordered native soldiers to bite the animal fat off bullets before inserting them into the Enfield rifles. This lack of cultural savvy caused a revolt among the Hindus and the believers in this religion, and the end of the East India Company's rule in 1858.

Ninety-seven percent of Pakistanis are followers of this religion.

This religion includes five pillars or main practices of the faith: profession of faith in the one God and in Muhammad as his Prophet; prayer five times a day; the giving of alms to the poor; fasting during the month of Ramadan; and the hajj, or pilgrimage to Mecca.

Followers of this religion believe the prophet Muhammad was the last and most perfect of God's messengers who include Adam, Abraham, Moses, Jesus, and others.

The Koran or Qur'an is the sacred scripture of this religion and is considered by believers to be the infallible word of God.

Buddhism

The religion that encourages people to follow The Middle Way—a path of balance rather than extremism.

Born a prince, Siddhartha Gautama, the founder of this religion, was born in the sixth century and through meditation attained the title, "Enlightened One."

This religion started as a movement of reform against the caste system and the domination of Brahmins in the practices of Hinduism.

The first of the four noble truths of this religion is that life always incorporates suffering. This can be the feeling you experience when you encounter pain, old age, sickness, loss, or separation from loved ones, but it can also represent a general unsatisfied feeling.

The Noble Eightfold path of this religion is Right Understanding, Right Intent, Right Speech, Right Action, Right Livelihood, Right Effort, Right Mindfulness, and Right Concentration.

Jainism

This religion doesn't have a single founder, but includes the oldest continuous monastic tradition in India. The truth has been revealed at different times by a tirthankara, which means a teacher who shows the way.

Mahavira is regarded as the man who gave this religion its present-day form.

The messages important in this religion are non-violence (Ahimsa), truth (Satya), non-stealing (Achaurya), celibacy (Brahma-charya), and non-possession (Aparigraha).

Among the five vows of this religion, non-violence (Ahimsa) is the cardinal principle, and hence it is called the highest religious principle, or the cornerstone.

According to this religion, all living beings are equal. No living being has a right to harm, injure, or kill any other living being, including animals, insects, and plants. Every living being has a right to exist and it is necessary to live with every other living being in perfect harmony and peace.

Hinduism

The predominant religion of India.

Life in this world is believed to be part of an eternal cycle of births and rebirths. What people do in the way of good or evil influences how they will be reborn after death.

Believers long for the eventual union of their soul with the world-soul, thereby breaking free from the cycle of births and rebirths.

The good life consists of moral behavior, service to others, seeking knowledge, worship, and devotion to one's personal deity who helps in the struggle with evil.

This was Gandhi's religion.

Sikhism

A monotheistic religion of India founded about 1500 CE by Guru Nanak, teaching the "Oneness of God," whose name is TRUTH. Nine Gurus followed him, who reinforced and added to what was taught by the first Guru.

Located in Amritsar opposite the Golden Temple, Akal Takht is the chief center of religious authority for Indian followers of this religion. In 1984 Indira Gandhi ordered the army to move into the Golden Temple complex at Amritsar, with the intent of crushing the militants hiding inside the temple; some 450 died in the fighting.

Punjab is the only Indian state with a majority of followers of this religion.

This religion encompasses a code of five virtues (truthfulness in living, contentment, patience, faith in the great teacher Nanak, and compassion) and five vices (lust, anger, greed, excessive attachment to any earthly object or person, and pride).

Male followers of this religion traditionally wear five signs of their faith: a short dagger symbolizing self-defense; unshorn hair symbolizing faith; a comb in the hair to show cleanliness; a bracelet, binding one symbolically to the truth; and a special undergarment symbolizing purity.

APPENDIX G
VOICES FROM KASHMIR (BBC)

Ishaq Khan, 55, is a professor of history who teaches at Kashmir University, Srinagar. He has written several books including *Kashmir's Transition to Islam*. He is currently compiling an encyclopedia on Sufis in South Asia. Dr. Khan is married to an English teacher.

As far as I am concerned, I am rooted in Kashmir. My identity as a Kashmiri is very central to my thinking and my writing. In fact, in 1992 I was in Oxford University for eight months and I had the option of settling down in the UK. But I did not. I returned home. I felt then that Kashmir was burning and I had to do something for my land. Since 1992 I have been reflecting on my identity and on the wonder that was Kashmir. The events of the past few years have been very, very painful.

Kashmir has been torn apart. Soon after my return I was so depressed and upset by the violence around me that I retreated into myself and tried to shut out everything around me. To calm myself and to find solace I turned to the Koran and would recite some verses every day. Since then I have embarked on writing a history of Kashmir. I have written about 100 pages. For my research, I have been traveling across the state.

One development, however, has disturbed me more than others. Wherever I go now in my travels, I feel that something is missing. I remember neighbourhoods which were inhabited by my Kashmiri Hindu brothers. They used to invite us to major Hindu festivals, such as Shivratri. And we, in turn, used to invite them to celebrate Eid. But now they are gone. Soon after the outbreak of violence in 1989, many Kashmiri Hindus left Srinagar and the Kashmir Valley, driven out of their homes in fear. I feel that I have lost something. It is my strong belief that without the Kashmiri Hindus one cannot talk about Kashmiri identity, or Kashmir. This is because it is their land. We, the Kashmiri Muslims, are converts [to Islam]. And it is the Kashmiri Hindus who have understood us best just as we understand them.

Kashmiri Hindus form about 5 to 6 percent of the total population of Kashmir and the Muslims form about 95 percent. But what sustains my belief that Kashmir is incomplete without its Hindus is the fact that we have lived together for six centuries amicably, without shedding blood. One of the great Kashmiri kings even got the classic Indian epic, *The Mahabharata*, and other ancient Sanskrit texts translated into Persian.

I am currently compiling an encyclopedia of Sufis in South Asia. During my work I have come across manuscripts written by Kashmiri Hindus which talk of the oneness of God, the one Creator who belongs to all and does not distinguish between Hindus and Muslims.

Religious Tolerance

Now one hears that there is some thought being given to the division of Kashmir along religious lines as a possible solution to our problem. In 1848 the princely state of Jammu and Kashmir came into being when it was placed under the rule of the Hindu Dogra kings.

In 1946, when an uprising against the king got going, some Kashmiri freedom fighters had advocated the splitting up of the state along religious lines. If it had taken place then, maybe it would have worked. But for this demand to be raised now would lead to, in my opinion, a second partition.

One of the distinctive features of Kashmir has been its religious tolerance. It used to be an ideal state where you would find Hindus, Muslims, and Buddhists all living together. And this ethos of co-existence has continued, despite the partition of the state in 1948 between India and Pakistan. For Kashmir to retain its sanity and for any hope for future generations, it is very important that this ethos is resurrected. It is the very basis of this land and without it we stand a very strong chance of losing our sense of who we are.

Sajjad Lone, 35, took over leadership of the separatist People's Conference party after his father, Abdul Ghani Lone, was assassinated in May 2002. He has studied in Britain and has a degree in Psychology. He also has business interests in Dubai. He is married to Asma, the daughter of Amanullah Khan, who heads the separatist Jammu and Kashmir Liberation Front in Pakistan-administered Kashmir.

I head the Jammu and Kashmir People's Conference which is part of the All Party Hurriyat Conference [the main separatist alliance]. Before entering politics I was a businessman and I used to also write articles in major Pakistani and Indian newspapers on issues confronting the region. I suppose you could say that I was analytically inclined towards politics. I am proud to be a Kashmiri.

Before 1989, we were living in a region where violence was a regular feature everywhere but in Kashmir. The crime rate here was almost zero. Killing or murders were unheard of. We were a peaceful society which was pure but not primitive. The brand of Islam that we followed was very liberal—in fact we were a very liberal society.

But in 1989 something went drastically wrong—and I think it was the way India handled Kashmir. Until then people had political grievances but they used political means to express their grievances. Somehow that movement switched from being political to becoming violent. The catalyst was the 1987 election in Kashmir, which was shamelessly and blatantly rigged. I think that became a turning point.

But the basic cause of the violence is rooted in history, when India pledged in 1948 to hold a plebiscite where the people of Kashmir would be free to choose to join India or Pakistan or become independent. They reneged on that promise and did not allow the plebiscite to be held. Over a period of time they brushed the problem under the carpet—India did not even allow any alternative solution to be considered. But it all erupted in 1989 after the elections two years earlier and a host of other factors.

The only way forward now is talks and only talks. If there were a military imbalance between India and Pakistan, that is, one country was militarily superior to the other, I, as a Kashmiri, would advocate a military solution. But the reality is that there is military parity between India and Pakistan and that is working against us. There is little chance of either country emerging as an outright victor in a conventional war, which means Kashmir will continue to be on the boil. It suits both countries.

So at the end of the day we all have to go to the negotiating table—India, Pakistan, and the Kashmiris. And the sooner we do this the better it is for all of us—the number of casualties will come down for a start. Every day that we delay talks we add at least eighteen to twenty people to the list of casualties. And it will keep multiplying. Even if we disagree with each other we should talk. If we are really sincere in our resolve to find a solution we might just find something in between which will not be in consonance with everybody's stated position. The new millennium has posed new challenges and offered fresh solutions and creative ways forward.

All of us want to go back to the Kashmir that was, the Kashmir of peace. It is my dream that the average Kashmiri, irrespective of his political future, should be equipped with the tools to face the challenges of the new era, the new market. We are as talented and as creative and as capable as anybody else. We just need a chance and we need to be given that opportunity.

Radhakrishnan, 74, is a Kashmir Hindu migrant who has been living in a refugee camp in Jammu for the past thirteen years. Originally from the border district of Kupwara, in the Kashmir Valley, he fled along with hundreds of thousands of Kashmiri Hindus after a sharp increase in separatist violence in 1989. He lives with his wife, two sons, and their wives in a tiny one-room house on the outskirts of Jammu.

I left the Kashmir Valley, and my home, thirteen years ago. My family used to live in Kupwara, not very far from the Line of Control. Despite being so close to Pakistan, we never had any problems.

I was eighteen years old in 1947, when all the trouble over our state erupted. We lived with our Muslim neighbours with little to fear. But in 1989 all that changed. As the violence broke out in the valley, we became increasingly insecure. People who we had lived with for years suddenly turned their backs on us.

Our neighbours told us not to worry—not to think of leaving. But they also said they would be unable to intervene if outsiders came to attack us. Young men, who I had seen grow up from the time they were little boys, began threatening us. They wanted to declare an Islamic state, they said. It was quite clear that there would be no place for us.

Life in the Camp

When the violence began spreading, and some people we knew became targets, we decided to leave. That's how I came to stay here in Jammu. We left everything behind. Our home, our possessions, everything. Soon after we left we heard our house had been burnt down by militants.

Life here in this camp is unbearable. The government has provided us with one-room homes. I used to live in a two-storey house. We had rich farmland and a little shop as well. But now my wife and I share a room with our sons and their wives. We have no room to cook, no place to change. We cannot entertain guests. It's uncivilised. When my wife or my daughters-in-law want to change clothes they go outside and use a dark corner in the alley—this is how we have lived for the past thirteen years.

Elections have been declared and we are being asked to cast our vote. In all these past years, in previous elections, I haven't seen a single candidate. Nobody has come here to ask us to cast our vote for them. That's how much they care for us. The point is that there is no political leader we can trust and who has the vision to take us out of this misery.

What we need is a visionary—a saint to lead us out of this darkness. Someone who is pure inside so that his deeds are clean. We are constantly being told by Kashmiri politicians that we should return to our homes, that it is safe to do so. These same leaders travel around in bulletproof cars with armed bodyguards because they are afraid they'll get killed by militants. The day they think it is safe to move around without all that protection is the day I'll consider moving back. Not before.

Kashmir is My Home

I've heard that some people are thinking of carving up our homeland and creating a small place for us Hindus. Maybe that's best—we live separately from the Kashmiri Muslims since we have nothing in common anymore. But it also makes me sad to think that this is what it's come to. I was born in Kashmir—it's my home. Why should I be asked to go away? Why can't I die there?

(From BBC News at bbcnews.com)

APPENDIX H
QUOTATIONS FROM HOLY BOOKS

Directions: The following statements are all from a Holy Book. Indicate if the source is: (A) the Old Testament; (B) the New Testament; or (C) the Qur'an.

___ 1. And We said: O Adam! Dwell thou and thy wife in the Garden, and eat ye freely of the fruits thereof where ye will; but come not near this tree lest ye become wrongdoers.

___ 2. O Children of Israel! Remember My favor wherewith I favored you and how I preferred you to all creatures.

___ 3. And remember when We deliver you from Pharaoh's folk, who were afflicting you with dreadful torment slaying your sons and sparing your women.

___ 4. We believe in God and that which is revealed unto us and that which was revealed unto Abraham, and Ishmael, and Isaac, and Jacob, and the tribes, and that which Moses and Jesus received, and that which the prophets received from their Lord.

___ 5. And when the angels said: O Mary! Lo! God hath chosen thee and made thee pure, and hath preferred thee above all the women of creation.

___ 6. And when We did appoint for Moses forty nights of solitude, and then ye chose the calf, when he had gone from you, and were wrongdoers.

___ 7. And I come confirming that which was before me of the Torah, and to make lawful some of that which was forbidden unto you. I come unto you with a sign from your Lord, so keep your duty to God and obey me.

___ 8. She said: My Lord! How can I have a child when no mortal has touched me? He said: So it will be! God createth what He will.

___ 9. And remember when the angel said: O Mary! Lo! God giveth thee glad tidings of a word from Him, whose name is the Messiah, Jesus, son of Mary, illustrious in the world and the hereafter, and one of those brought near unto God.

___ 10. One among them said: Kill not Joseph, but if ye must be doing, fling him into the depth of the pit. Some caravan will find him.

Answer Key:

The source for all ten statements is the Qur'an.   *(Adapted from an exercise prepared by Mounir Farrah.)*

APPENDIX I
DOCUMENTARY SPECIAL ON INDIA & PAKISTAN
CLASS TASKS

Learners who are willing to become involved at a different level beyond simply listening to "a presentation" process information and issues at a new depth. The following tasks are homework assignments for research, organizing information, preparation, and creative presentation to the rest of the class in the format of a TV documentary on India and Pakistan. The "documentary" will "air" during the last class session. Encourage everyone to get involved, individually or as a team.

News Clips

The study leader may choose the articles or portions of articles and can use multiples of these news clips according to class size and time.

You are a highly-paid, talented TV reporter who has uncovered information about _____. Use an excerpt from one of the articles in *Response* magazine that highlights India/Pakistan for your information. Develop a clip for the evening news. Remember that TV news programs are tightly planned. Your clip can be no more than four minutes long. Time it carefully! You may draft others from the class to help you with this assignment, for example, you may want to "interview" someone in your clip.

Thumbs Up

The children's curriculum for the India/Pakistan study will be available in 2006. Review this resource for the class. You have four minutes.

You Are There—E. Stanley Jones

Create and give a first-person account of E. Stanley Jones, missionary extraordinaire. You only have four minutes, so choose details that you find most important and interesting from the Internet site, *http://ashram.modular.institute.com/site/Templates/template4.aspx?tabindex=1&tabid=67*.

Editorial Analysis

Your assignment is to analyze how Gandhi influenced Martin Luther King, Jr. Use the quotes from Dr. Martin Luther King, Jr. in Appendix C, Quotable Quotes (p. 170). You could also do an online search for other writings of Dr. King. Limit your analysis to four minutes.

Exposé and Action

Briefly report (no more than four minutes) on child workers and what can be done to stop this terrible problem. Use the Rugmark website for your research: *http://www.rugmark.org/help.htm*.

Mission Update

If you have persons in your class who have visited India or Pakistan, have participated in a volunteer in mission project there, or have special expertise, ask them to give a brief report on what's happening (your call on time).

APPENDIX J
A DIALOGUE BETWEEN
ISABELLA THOBURN AND CLARA SWAIN

(An Imaginary Meeting in 1900)

Clara: Isabella, how good is it to see you again. How are you?

Isabella: Oh, I'm quite well, thank you. It's very fulfilling at the end of one's life to look back and realize what an exciting adventure we both had in India, as women serving women.

Clara: How true, how true! It seems like only yesterday when we both felt called to serve the Christ in far-off lands, and yet, not being married, we had little opportunity for that to happen.

Isabella: Ah yes! If it hadn't been for that small band of visionary women in Boston who formed the Women's Foreign Mission Society of the Methodist Episcopal Church, we never would have been able to serve our Lord in India. Do you remember your journey to India?

Clara: Oh, it was horrible. It's a good thing that I had my faith in God to see me through. The latter part of our voyage was very rough and I was too sick to write, and I had five sick ones to look after besides myself. I cannot bear to think of the sea, it treated me so badly. When I finally arrived in Bareilly, my luggage and precious cargo of medicines didn't arrive until a month later. But my medical work really began the day of my arrival. When I came out of my room in the morning, I found a company of native Christian women and girls eagerly awaiting the appearance of the "Doctor Miss Sahiba," and with the aid of a good missionary sister I was able to understand their words of welcome and find out what I could do to help them. As I had no medicines with me, I procured a few simple remedies for their ailments from Mrs. Thomas.

Isabella: How wonderful that our Lord provides grace sufficient for all our needs!

Clara: Oh, yes. By the end of the year I had treated 1,300 patients and trained seventeen medical students. I lectured in anatomy, physiology, and diseases of women and children. By 1874, I had built a

Women's Hospital and Medical School, the first in all of Asia. The land for the hospital was another way that our gracious God provides for our needs.

Isabella: What do you mean?

Clara: The Nawab of Rampore was a Muslim who had sworn never to allow another Christian missionary in his city. A missionary friend and I prayed about our problem, and then approached the Nawab. Miracle of miracles, when he found out we needed the land for a hospital for women, he gave it to us and said, "Take it, take it; I give it to you with much pleasure for that purpose." You see, religious customs prohibited male doctors from caring for women, and the Nawab could see the great need.

Isabella: Yes, the rules of men were often directed against the good of women and children. I remember when I opened a school for girls in India in the Lucknow bazaar. The young women were so frightened of going against those rules that I had to hire a man with a club to guard the door of the school. Someone once said that women in India were "unwanted at birth, unhonoured in life, unwept in death."

Clara: Your push for the education of women certainly helped give them a sense of empowerment and worth.

Isabella: Surely, surely! One of the women I trained was Lilavati Singh, a beautiful and cultivated representative of the upper caste. She toured America pleading for funds to expand the educational work that we had begun. President Harrison remarked after meeting her, that if she alone had been the result of all the money spent on missions, she was worth the entire sum.

Clara: I hope and pray that women in the future will understand the need and continue to support what we have begun.

Isabella: Amen to that, sister!

(Adapted from material found at
http://www.gospelcom.net/chi/DAILYF/2001/01/daily-01-20-2001.shtml
and *http://www.gospelcom.net/chi/DAILYF/2002/01/daily-01-07-2002.shtml*.)

NOTES

Introduction

1. Taken from the May 12, 2003 service of worship of the Mutuality of Mission Committee, National Council of Churches of Christ in the U.S.A., held in Toronto, Canada.

Chapter 1

1. "Along the Missouri, Life Ebbs and Flows," *The New York Times,* Vol. CL 11. No. 52, 501 (June 1, 2003): A1 and A32.

2. Brahman is beyond all duality. Therefore he is *advaita* (without duality). He is without qualities (*nirguna*); without differences (*nivisesa*); without conditions (*nirpadhi*). Experience with Brahman is a non-dual experience. See the United Methodist Mission Study book for 2003, *Creating Interfaith Community*, by R. Marston Speight with Study Guides by the Dharmarajes, pages 21–24 for a basic understanding of Hinduism. See the resources listed on page 90 for a further understanding of the presence of various religions in the immigrant communities in the United States.

3. Moazziz Ali, "Hindutva vs. Hinduism," 35–36.

4. "Im Orient mussen wir das hochste Romantische suchen." Quoted in Romila Thapar in *Ancient Indian Social History: Some Interpretations* (Delhi, India: Oxford University Press, 1987): 45-82. Also in Edward Said's *Orientalism* (New York: Vintage Books, 1979): 98.

5. Taken from Richard Lannoy's *Speaking Tree: A Study on Indian Culture and Society* (New Delhi: Oxford University Press, 1971): 308.

6. Ofelia Ortega's "Peace in the City" in *Ecumenical Review*, Vol. 55:3 (July 2003).

7. Nelle Morton.

8. See Betty Heiman's *Facets of Indian Thought* (George and Unwin: London, 1964). Quoted in *The Speaking Tree* by Richard Lannoy (Oxford University Press, New Delhi, 1971): 278.

9. For a similar phrase, see John V. Taylor's book, *The Go Between God: The Holy Spirit & the Christian Mission* (New York: Oxford University Press Inc., 1972).

10. The God who makes differences complementary to each other, thereby enhancing the beauty in variety and diversity.

Chapter 2

1. Quoted in *We Drink from Our Own Wells: A Spiritual Journey of a People* by Gustavo Gutierrez (Maryknoll, New York: Orbis Books, 1997): 164.

2. John C. B. Webster in *The Dalit Christians: A History* (Delhi, India: ISPCK, 1992): 34.

3. K. V. Paul Pillai in *India's Search for the Unknown Christ* (New Delhi, India: Sabina Printing Press, 1979): 156-158.

4. Richard Fox Young in "Some Hindu Perspectives on Christian Missionaries in the Indic World of the Mid-Nineteenth Century" in *Christians, Cultural Interactions, and India's Religious Traditions.* Eds., Judith M. Brown and Robert Eric Frykenberg (Grand Rapids, Michigan: William B. Eerdmans Publishing Company, 2002): 40.

5. Quoted by Theodore W. Jennings, Jr., in *Good News to the Poor: John Wesley's Evangelical Economics* (1990): 80-81.

6. Alice G. Knotts in *Fellowship of Love: Methodist Women Changing American Racial Attitudes* 1920–1968 (Nashville, Tennessee: Abingdon Press, 1996): 219.

7. "The Thirteenth Rock Edict" quoted in *Indian History.* Civil Service Examinations. Ed. V. K. Agnihotri. 19th edition (New Delhi: Allied Publishers, 2003): A-249.

Chapter 3

1. John N. Hollister. *The Centenary of the Methodist Church in Southern Asia* (Lucknow, India: Lucknow Publishing House, 1956): 334. James K. Mathews. *South of the Himalayas: One Hundred Years of Methodism in India and Pakistan* (Nashville: The Parthenon Press, 1955): 135-136.

2. For some of the facts leading to a separate nation, see *Pakistan, its People, its Society, its Culture* by Donald N. Wilbur (New Haven: Hraf Press, 1964): 21; *India and Pakistan: A Political Analysis* by Hugh Tinker (New York: Praeger, 1962): 23-25; *The Clash of Fundamentalism: Crusades, Jihads and Modernity* by Tariq Ali (London & New York: Verso, 2002): 9-10.

3. Report of the Court of Inquiry constituted under Punjab Act II of 1954 to enquire into Punjab disturbances of 1953, Lahore 1954. See work under "Munir Report." Quoted in Hugh Tinker's *India and Pakistan: A Political Analysis* (New York: Praeger, 1962): 74.

4. For the U.N. Resolutions on the Indo-Pakistan issue of Kashmir, see Web Resources, pp. 203-204.

5. Quoted by M. J. Akbar in *Kashmir: Behind the Vale* (Karan Press, New Delhi, 2002): 223.

6. For a map of United Nations Peacekeeping Force Mission in the Jammu/Kashmir region (UNMOGIP), visit: *http://www.un.org/Depts/Cartographic/map/dpko/unmogip.pdf*.

7. "Reaching Critical Will Fact Sheet," *www.reachingcriticalwill.org*.

8. Ibid.

9. Visit *http://ncccusa.org/news/news44.html* for a statement by the Rev. Dr. Joan B. Campbell adopted by the National Council of Churches on "India's Testing Nuclear Weapons."

10. "Reaching Critical Will Fact Sheet," *www.reachingcriticalwill.org*.

11. Ibid.

Chapter 4

1. John N. Hollister (see chapter 3, note 1 above), 3.

2. Hollister, 5.

3. Ibid.

4. Mary Isham in *Valorous Ventures: A Record of Sixty and Six Years of the Woman's Foreign Missionary Society, Methodist Episcopal Church* (Boston: WFMS, 1926): 18.

5. Dana Robert in *American Women in Mission: A Social History of Their Thought and Practice* (Macon, Georgia: Mercer University Press, 1998): 126.

6. *Human Development Report in South Asia 2000: The Gender Question*, Mahbub ul Haq Human Development Center. (Oxford, England: Oxford University Press, 2000): 105.

7. *Human Development Report in South Asia 2000*: 113.

8. J. M. Thoburn in *Life of Isabella Thoburn* (Cincinnati, Ohio: Jennings and Pye, 1903): 291.

9. Marjorie A. Dimmit in *Isabella Thoburn College: A Record from its Beginnings to its Diamond Jubilee*, 1961 (Cincinnati, Ohio: World Outlook Press, 1963): 11.

10. Mary Isham (see note 4 above): 18.

11. Videotaped interview with Dr. Sunita Charles, Principal of Isabella Thoburn College, India, on June 16, 2004.

12. Ibid.

13. Ibid.

14. Information on Kinnaird College is based on *The Century of the Methodist Church in Southern Asia* by John N. Hollister (Lucknow, India: The Lucknow Publishing House, 1956): 133. Also *Celebrating Kinnaird: Pioneering Women's Education in the Punjab* by Vivienne Stacey. The Association of Kinnaird College for Women. (Lahore, Pakistan: Allied Press [Pvt.] Ltd., 2002).

15. Telephone interview with Dr. Mira Phailbus on August 12, 2003 by Glory Dharmaraj.

16. Ibid.

17. Information taken from Joyce D. Sohl's "Education as Mission" and update on "Connections" in *Communique: Women in Higher Education* (Women's Division, General Board of Global Ministries, August 2003): 1-5.

18. Interview, April 8, 2004.

19. John N. Hollister (see chapter 3, note 1 above): 75.

20. For more information, visit *www.vellorecmc.org*.

21. See Mabelle and Rajanikant Arole's *Jamkhed: A Comprehensive Rural Health Project* (London: The Macmillan Press Ltd., 1994).

22. Information from Dr. Cherian Thomas, Executive Secretary for Health and Welfare of the General Board of Global Ministries of The United Methodist Church.

23. Salman Masood in "Pakistani Inquiry Reveals Details of a Woman's Honor Killing" in *The New York Times* December 14, 2003: 15.

24. *Human Development Report in South Asia 2000: The Gender Question*. The Mahbub ul Haq Development Centre. (Oxford: Oxford University Press, 2000): 92.

25. *Human Development Report in South East Asia: The Gender Question*, 99.

26. In *Women and Society in Ancient India* edited by S. Vats and Sakuntala Mudgal, Om Publications, Faridabad, India, 1999 (p. 26), the authors list the eight different forms of marriage in the *Rig Veda*, the earliest work of Hindu literature between BCE 2500–1500. They are the "brahma," where the father himself gives his daughter as a gift, along with other gifts of jewels, to a man to marry; the "daiva," where the girl is married to a priest who presides over a sacrifice during the course of its performance; the "arsha," where the bridegroom offers a cow and a bull or two pairs of them to the bride's father; the "prajapatya," where the father of the bride addresses the couple with the text,

"May both of you perform your duties"; the "asura," where the bridegroom willingly gives as much wealth as he desires to the bride and her family; the "gandharva," which is the voluntary union of a young woman and man; the "rakshasa," where the bride is forcibly carried from her home; and the "paishacha," where a man by stealth seduces a girl who is asleep, intoxicated or not in a good frame of mind. Gradually, the last one came to be condemned categorically. The first four were allowed for a Brahmin. Some say that the seventh form was allowed in the case of Kshatriyas, warriors. But the members of the current Indian History Congress state that to list "rakshasa marriage" as a "legitimate" form of marriage in the past, especially in children's text books, is a distortion of the past. See "Debate on Distortions" by Parvathi Menon in *Frontline* (January 30, 2004. Vol. 21:2): 41.

27. "A Synopsis of the Report of the National Committee on the Status of Women in India."

28. Human Development Report in South Asia 2000, 121.

29. Ibid.

30. Ibid., 122.

31. For the perspective of a non-Christian scholar, see Maina Chawla Singh's book, *Gender, Religion, and "Heathen Lands": American Missionary Women in South Asia, 1860s–1940s* (New York: Garland, 2000). She finds in her research a balance between post-colonial writings on Western imperialism and the loving records and narratives of women alumnae of missionary colleges and schools.

32. *The Hindu Scriptures, Rig Veda X.* Trans. R. C. Zaehner (London: J. M. Dent, 1966): 90.

33. *National Geographic* published a special issue on "India's Untouchables" in June 2003.

34. A. M. Abraham Ayrookuzhiel, "The Ideological Nature of the Emerging Dalit Consciousness" in *Towards a Common Dalit Ideology*, ed. Arvind P. Nirmal: 88.

35. Quoted in a paper presented by Aruna Gnanadason in *Towards a Common Dalit Ideology*, ed. Arvind P. Nirmal (Madras, India: Nandan Offset, 1989), 110.

36. James K. Mathews in *South of the Himalayas: One Hundred Years of Methodism in India and Pakistan* (Nashville: Parthenon Press, 1955): 91-92.

37. J. Tremayne Copplestone in *History of Methodist Missions*. Vol. 4 (New York: General Board of Global Ministries, 1973): 1155.

38. Bangalore, India, January 7, 2004.

39. First person narration is based on a report given in *Pan on Fire: Eight Dalit Women Tell their Story*. Indian Social Institute, New Delhi, 1988. Quoted in Aruna Gnanadason in *Towards A Common Dalit Ideology*, ed. Arvind P. Nirmal: 109.

40. Lalrinawmi Ralte in "Doing Tribal Women's Theology," *In God's Image*, Vol. 19, No. 4. December 2000: 2-4.

41. Shim Shimray in his "Human Rights Violation in Northeast India with Reference to Armed Forces (Special Powers) Act, 1958," *In God's Image* Vol. 19. No. 4, December 2000: 5-11.

42. Interview on January 16, 2004, in Bangalore, India.

43. Lalsangkima Pachuau talks about the impact of mission on Northeast India in his article, "Church-Mission Dynamics in Northeast India" (154-161) in *International Bulletin of Missionary Research*, Vol. 27. No. 4: October 2003.

44. Lalrinawmi Ralte in "A Handful of Rice—Metaphor for Mizo Women's Power," *In God's Image*, Vol. 19, No. 4. December 2000: 41-44. See Appendix F for the song, "A Handful of Rice."

45. *The Small Hands of Slavery: Bonded Child Labor in India* (New York: Human Rights Watch, 1996).

46. For more about this "Innovative CWS Quilt-Making Program Means Income for Afghanistan Refugee Women," visit *http://ncccusa.org/news/01news110.htm*.

47. For a more detailed analysis, see James B. Martin-Schramm's *Population Perils and the Churches' Response* (Geneva: WCC, 1997).

48. Interview with Dorothy Sampathkumar on April 7, 2004.

Chapter 5

1. Kaj Baago, *Pioneers of Indigenous Christianity*, (Bangalore: CLS, 1969), 12.

2. See Waskom Pickett, *Christian Mass Movements in India*, (Cincinnati: Abingdon Press, 1933).

3. V. S. Azariah's "The Problem of Cooperation Between Foreign and Native Workers" in *Roots of the Great Mission Debate in Mission: Mission in Historical and Theological Perspective*, ed. Roger E. Hedlund, (Bangalore, India: Theological Book Trust, 1984): 48.

4. Bengt Sundkler, *Church of South India: The Movement Towards Union 1900-1947*, (London: Lutterworth Press, 1954): 101.

5. A phone interview by Glory Dharmaraj with James Matthews and Eunice James Matthews on March 31, 2004.

6. Gavin D'Costa, *Dialogue and Alliance*, Vol. 2, No. 2. Summer 1988.

7. James K. Mathews in *South of the Himalayas*, 128.

8. Ada Maria Isasi-Diaz coined the phrase "kin-dom" instead of kingdom to convey the concept of "kingdom of God" in a post-colonial, feminist context.

9. Interview at the General Board of Global Ministries of The United Methodist Church on April 2, 2004.

10. Interview by Glory Dharmaraj with Dr. Evangeline Anderson Rajkumar.

11. Interview by Glory Dharmaraj with Dr. Monica Melanchthon.

12. For more on Dalit theology, see *Eyes That Can See: A Way of Reading the Bible from Dalit Perspective*, by Daniel Monodeep (2004). These Bible studies by a pastor in the Church of North India give an understanding of emerging Dalit scholarship. Available from the Centre for Dalit/Subaltern Studies, House No. 181, Sector 1, Phase 1, Pocket 1, Dwarka, New Delhi, India. The cost is $4.00 U.S. plus postage from the above address.

13. *The Times of India*, December 13, 1995. Bombay edition. Quoted by C. V. Matthew in his article, "Hindutva: Majority Religious Nationalism in India" (212-237) in *Mission in Context: Missiological Reflections*. Essays in Honor of Roger and June Hedlund. Ed. C. V. Matthew. (New Delhi, India: ISPCK): 234.

14. *The Hindu*, December 28, 2003: 3.

15. *Ecumenical Considerations for Dialogue and Relations with People of Other Religions* (Geneva: WCC Publications, 2003): 4.

16. For a "Letter from the National Council of Churches in the USA Deploring Minority Attacks in India," see *http://ncccusa.org/news/99news27.html*.

17. Testimony of Bishop Rumalshah before the Senate Foreign Relations Committee in the United States on June 17, 1998.

Chapter 6

1. See Glory Dharmaraj's *Concepts of Mission* (New York: General Board of Global Ministries, 1999): 59.

2. *USA Today* (March 25, 2004): 3B.

3. Suleman Din in *India Abroad* (New York: May 23, 2003) Vol. XXXIII, No. 34: A 6.

4. For more information, go to *www.claasfamily.org*.

5. United Methodist Women's Action Alert on "Fundamentalism: A Barrier to Peace and Justice," Office of Public Policy, Spring 2004.

6. United Nations Commission on Human Rights, 59th Session (March-April 2003), Item 11(a) of the Provisional Agenda. Written statement submitted by the Commission of Churches on International Affairs of the World Council of Churches. "Civil and Political Rights Including the Question of Religious Intolerance." May 11, 2004: 2-3.

7. "Action Alert: Patriot Act Update" (June 2004) by the Office of Public Policy, Women's Division, General Board of Global Ministries.

8. Letter sent out by the South Asian Youth Leadership Team on April 23, 2004.

9. Glory Dharmaraj's phone interview with Clement John on May 5, 2004.

10. Phone interview with Frances Major, retired missionary, at Brooks-Howell Home, Asheville, North Carolina, April 8, 2004.

Epilogue

1. E. Stanley Jones in *Gandhi: Portrayal of a Friend* (Nashville, 1993): 152-153.

BIBLIOGRAPHY

Agnihortri, V. K., ed. *Indian History* 19th edition. New Delhi, India: Allied Publishers, 2003.

Akbar, M.J. *Kashmir: Behind the Vale*. New Delhi, India: Karan Press, 2002.

Ali, Tariq. *The Clash of Fundamentalism: Crusade, Jihads and Modernity*. London and New York: Verso, 2002.

Arole, Mabelle and Rajanikant. *Jakmkhed: A Comprehensive Rural Health Project*. London: The Macmillan Press Ltd., 1994.

Ayrookuzhiel, A. M. Abraham. "The Ideological Nature of the Emerging Dalit Consciousness." 81-95. *Toward a Common Dalit Ideology*. Arvind P. Nirmal, ed. Gurukul Lutheran Theological College and Research Institute. Madras: Nandan Offset, 1989.

Azariah, V. S. "The Problem of Cooperation Between Foreign and Native Workers." *Roots of the Great Mission Debate in Mission: Mission in Historical and Theological Perspective*. Roger E. Headlund, ed. Bangalore, India: Theological Book Trust, 1984.

Baago, Kaj. *Pioneers of Indigenous Christianity*. Bangalore: Christian Literature Service, 1969.

Brown, Judith M. and Frykenberg, Robert Eric, eds. *Christians, Cultural Interactions, and India's Religious Traditions*. Grand Rapids, MI: William B. Eerdmans Publishing Co., 2002.

Copplestone, Tremayne. *History of Methodist Missions*. Vol. 4. New York: General Board of Global Ministries, 1973.

Dharmaraj, Glory. *Concepts of Mission*. New York: General Board of Global Ministries, 1999.

Dimmit, Marjorie A. *Isabella Thoburn College: A Record from Its Beginning to Its Diamond Jubilee, 1961*. Cincinnati: World Outlook Press, 1963.

Din, Suleman. *India Abroad*. XXXIII:34. New York: May 23, 2003.

Egan, Timothy. "Along the Missouri, Life Ebbs and Flows." *New York Times*. CL 11:52. June 1, 2003, A1 and A32.

Gnanadason, Aruna. "Dalit Women: The Dalit of the Dalits." 109-120. *Towards a Common Dalit Ideology*. Arvind P. Nirmal, ed. Madras, India: Nandan Offset, 1989.

Guitierrez, Gustavo. *We Drink from Our Own Wells: A Spiritual Journey of a People*. Maryknoll, New York: Orbis Books, 1997.

Heiman, Betty. *Facets of Indian Thought*. London: George and Unwin, 1964.

Hindu, The. December 28, 2003.

Hollister, John N. *The Centenary of the Methodist Church in Southern Asia*. Lucknow, India: Lucknow Publishing House, 1956.

Human Development Report in South Asia 2000. Mahbub ul Haq Human Development Center. New York: Oxford University Press, 2000.

"Human Rights Watch." *The Small Hands of Slavery: Bonded Child Labor in India*. New York: Human Rights Watch, 1996.

Isham, Mary. *Valorous Ventures: A Record of Sixty and Six Years of the Woman's Foreign Missionary Society, Methodist Episcopal Church*. Boston: WFMS, 1926.

Jennings, Theodore W., Jr. *Good News to the Poor: John Wesley's Evangelical Economics*. Nashville: Abingdon Press, 1990.

Jones, Stanley E. *Gandhi: Portrayal of a Friend*. Nashville: Abingdon Press, 1948. Under the title, *Mahatma Gandhi—An Interpretation*, 1993.

Knotts. G. Alice. *Fellowship of Love: Methodist Women Changing American Racial Attitudes 1920–1968*. Nashville: Abingdon Press, 1996.

Lannoy, Richard. *Speaking Tree: A Study on Indian Culture and Society*. New Delhi, India: Oxford University Press, 1971.

Martin-Schramm, James B. *Population Perils and the Churches' Response*. Geneva: World Council of Churches, 1997.

Masood, Salman. "Pakistani Inquiry Reveals Details of a Woman's Honor Killing." *New York Times*. December 14, 2003.

Mathew, C. V., ed. "Hindutva: Majority Religious Nationalism in India." *Mission in Context: Missiological Reflections*. New Delhi, India: ISPCK, 2003.

Mathews, James K. *South of the Himalayas: One Hundred Years of Methodism.* Nashville: The Parthenon Press, 1955.

Menon, Parvathi. "Debate on Distortions." *Frontline.* 21:2. January 30, 1994.

Morton, Nelle. *The Journey is Home.* Boston: Beacon Press, 1985.

National Committee on the Status of Women, India, The. *A Synopsis of the Report.* 1975.

National Council of Churches in the U.S.A., The "India's Testing Nuclear Weapons." News Archives. May 15, 1998.

National Council of Churches in the U.S.A., The "Letter from the National Council of Churches in the U.S.A. Deploring Anti-Minority Attacks in India." News Archives. March 9, 1999.

National Council of Churches in the U.S.A., The "Innovative CWS Quilt-Making Program Means Income for Afghanistan Refugee Women." News Archives. December 3, 2001.

National Geographic. "India's Untouchables." June 2003.

Nirmal, Arvind P., ed. *Towards a Common Dalit Theology.* Gurukul Lutheran Theological College and Research Institute. Madras, India: Nandan Offset, 1989.

Ortega, Ofelia. "Peace in the City." *Ecumenical Review.* 55:3. July, 2003.

Pachau, Lalsangkima. "Church Mission Dynamics in Northeast India." *International Bulletin.* 27:4. October 2003.

Pickett, Waskom. *Christian Mass Movement in India.* Cincinnati: Abingdon Press, 1933.

Pillai, Paul K. V. *India's Search for the Unknown Christ.* New Delhi, India: Sabina Printing Press, 1979.

Ralte, Lalrinawmi. "Doing Tribal Women's Theology." 2-4. *In God's Image.* 19:4. December, 2000.

Ralte, Lalrinawmi. "A Handful of Rice—Metaphor for Mizo Women's Power." 41-44. *In God's Image.* 19:4. December, 2000.

Robert, Dana. *American Women in Mission: A Social History of Their Thought and Practice.* Macon, GA: Mercer University Press, 1998.

Rumalshah, Munawar. Testimony before Senate Foreign Relations Committee. June 17, 1998. "Being a Christian in Pakistan." *Hear the Cry: Standing in Solidarity with the Suffering Church.* Margaret Larom, ed. Anglican and Global Relations, ECUSA. New York, 1998.

Said, Edward. *Orientalism.* New York: Vintage Books, 1979.

Shimray, Shim. "Human Rights Violation in Northeast India with Reference to Armed Forces (Special Powers) Act, 1958." 5-11. *In God's Image. 19:4. December, 2000.*

Singh, Maina Chawla, ed. *Gender, Religion, and "Heathen Lands": American Missionary Women in South Asia. 1860s-1940s.* New York: Garland, 2000.

Sohl, Joyce. "Women in Higher Education." *Communiqué.* New York: Women's Division, General Board of Global Ministries. August 2003.

South Asian Youth Leadership Team. "Letter to the Churches." April 23, 2004.

Speight, R. Marston. *Creating Interfaith Community.* Study Guide. Glory and Jacob Dharmaraj. New York: General Board of Global Ministries, 2002.

Stacey, Vivienne. *Celebrating Kinnaird: Pioneering Women's Education in the Punjab.* Lahore, Pakistan: Allied Press (Pvt.) Ltd., 2002.

Sundkler, Bengt. *Church of South India: The Movement Towards Union 1900–1947.* London: Lutterworth Press, 1954.

Taylor, John V. *The Go Between God: The Holy Spirit and the Christian Mission.* New York: Oxford University Press, 1972.

Thapar, Romila. *Ancient Indian Social History: Some Interpretations.* Delhi, India: Oxford University Press, 1987.

Thoburn, J. M. *Life of Isabella Thoburn.* Cincinnati: Jennings & Pye, 1903.

Tinker, Hugh. *India and Pakistan: A Political Analysis.* New York: Praeger, 1962.

United Methodist Women's Action Alert. "Fundamentalism: A Barrier to Peace and Justice." Office of Public Policy. Spring 2004.

USA Today. March 25, 2004, 3B.

Vats, S. and Mudgal, Sakuntala, eds. *Women and Society in Ancient India.* Faridabad, India: Om Publications, 1999.

Webster, John C. B. *The Dalit Christians: A History*. Delhi, India: ISPK, 1992.

Wilbur, Donald N. *Pakistan, Its People, Its Society, Its Culture*. New Haven: Hraf Press, 1964.

Women's Division. General Board of Global Ministries. The United Methodist Church. "Action Alert: Patriot Act Update." Office of Public Policy. June 2004.

Women's Division. General Board of Global Ministries. The United Methodist Church. "Fundamentalism: A Barrier to Peace and Justice." Office of Public Policy. Spring 2004.

World Council of Churches. *Ecumenical Considerations for Dialogue and Relations with People of Other Religions*. Geneva: WCC Publications, 2003.

World Council of Churches. "United Nations Commission on Human Rights. 59th Session (March-April 2003). Item 11(a) of the Provisional Agenda." 2-3. Written statement by the Commission of Churches on International Affairs. May 11, 2004.

Young, Richard Fox. "Some Hindu Perspectives on Christian Missionaries in the Indic World of the Mid-Nineteenth Century." *Christians, Cultural Interactions and India's Religious Traditions*. Judith M. Brown and Robert Eric Frykenberg, eds. Grand Rapids: William B. Eerdmans Publishing Company, 2002.

Zaehner, R. C., trans. *The Hindu Scriptures, Rig Veda X: 90.* London: J. M. Dent, 1966.

INTERVIEWS BY GLORY DHARMARAJ

Gnanadson, Aruna. World Council of Churches. Geneva. Phone interview. May 5, 2004.

John, Clement. World Council of Churches. Phone interview. May 5, 2004.

Major, Frances. Retired Missionary at Brooks-Howell Retirement Home, Asheville, North Carolina. Phone interview. April 8, 2004.

Mathews, James and Eunice. Retired Missionaries. Phone interview. March 31, 2004.

Melanchthon, Monica. United Theological College (UTC), Bangalore, India. January 12, 2004.

Phailbus, Mira. Retired Principal, Kinnaird College, Pakistan. Phone interview. August 12, 2003.

Rajkumar, Evangeline Anderson. UTC, Bangalore, India. January 13, 2004.

Ralte, Lalrinawmi. UTC, Bangalore, India. January 16, 2004.

Sampathkumar, Dorothy. General Board of Global Ministries, The United Methodist Church, 475 Riverside Drive, New York. April 7, 2004.

VIDEOTAPED INTERVIEWS BY LANE WINN AND QUINN JOHNSON AT THE GENERAL BOARD OF GLOBAL MINISTRIES, NEW YORK

Charles, Sunita. Principal, Isabella Thoburn College, Lucknow, India. June 16, 2004.

Rumalshah, Munawar. General Secretary, The United Society for the Propagation of the Gospel. April 2, 2004.

WEB RESOURCES

For updates on India and Pakistan, for general information about online newspapers, visit: *http://allnewspapers.com*.

For specific information and news from India, visit the website for *The Times of India*: *http://timesofindia.indiatimes.com/cms.dll/xml/uncomp/default?*

For *The Pakistan Christian Post*, the official news information service of the Pakistan Congress, visit: *http://www.pakistanchristianpost.com*.

For information on the Church of North India, visit: *http://www.cnisynod.org/*.

For information on the Church of South India, visit: *http://www.csichurch.com/*.

For information on Mar Thoma Church, Diocese of North America and Europe, visit: *http://www.marthomachurch.com/indexnew.htm*.

For the National Council of Churches of Pakistan: Fax: 92-42-63-69745.

For information on Church Councils and Christian Conference in Asia, visit: *http://www.cca.org.hk/home1.htm*.

To read the United Nations Resolutions on Kashmir, visit:

http://www.kashmiri-cc.ca/un/sc17jan48.htm

http://www.kashmiri-cc.ca/un/sc20jan48.htm

http://www.kashmiri-cc.ca/un/sc6feb48.htm

http://www.kashmiri-cc.ca/un/sc21apr48.htm

http://www.kashmiri-cc.ca/un/sc3jun48.htm

http://www.kashmiri-cc.ca/un/sc13aug48.htm

http://www.kashmiri-cc.ca/un/sc5jan49.htm

http://www.kashmiri-cc.ca/un/sc22dec49.htm

http://www.kashmiri-cc.ca/un/sc14mar50.htm

http://www.kashmiri-cc.ca/un/sc30mar51.htm

http://www.kashmiri-cc.ca/un/sc10nov51.htm

http://www.kashmiri-cc.ca/un/sc23dec52.htm

http://www.kashmiri-cc.ca/un/sc24jan57.htm

http://www.kashmiri-cc.ca/un/sc14feb57.htm

http://www.kashmiri-cc.ca/un/sc21feb57.htm

http://www.kashmiri-cc.ca/un/sc16nov57.htm

http://www.kashmiri-cc.ca/un/sc2dec57.htm

http://www.kashmiri-cc.ca/un/sc22jun62.htm

http://www.kashmiri-cc.ca/un/sc18may64.htm

http://www.kashmiri-cc.ca/un/sc4sep65.htm

http://www.kashmiri-cc.ca/un/sc6sep65.htm

http://www.kashmiri-cc.ca/un/sc20sep65.htm

http://www.kashmiri-cc.ca/un/sc27sep65.htm

http://www.kashmiri-cc.ca/un/sc5nov65.htm

http://www.kashmiri-cc.ca/un/sc6dec71.htm

http://www.kashmiri-cc.ca/un/sc456dec71.htm

http://www.kashmiri-cc.ca/un/sc21dec71.htm

NOTES

NOTES

Glory E. Dharmaraj

Glory Dharmaraj is Executive Secretary for Justice Education for the Women's Division of the General Board of Global Ministries of The United Methodist Church. She directs the United Methodist Seminar Program on National and International Affairs at the Church Center for the United Nations in New York.

Glory spent her childhood on a tea estate in Sri Lanka. Completing her undergraduate and master's studies in India, she taught at Sarah Tucker College in Tamil Nadu, and Queen Mary's in Bombay. She received her Ph.D. from Loyola University of Chicago. She has done special studies at Harvard University. Currently she is completing her Doctor of Ministry, a joint program at San Francisco Theological Seminary, California, and Ecumenical Theological Education at the World Council of Churches, Geneva.

An author and co-author of many books, Glory is married to a United Methodist clergy person, and has served with him at churches in Bombay, Illinois Great Rivers, and New York Annual Conferences. Glory has taught at numerous regional and conference schools of Christian mission.

Diane M. Miller

Currently living in Pittsburgh, Pennsylvania, Diane Miller recently worked for the Women's Division as Executive Secretary for Schools and Mission Studies. Prior to moving to Pittsburgh, Diane lived at Olmsted Manor, an Adult Retreat/Renewal Center where she led retreats, presented mission programs, and interacted with adults seeking to grow spiritually and expand their understanding of mission.

The recipient of numerous state and national teaching awards when she worked with gifted students in northwestern Pennsylvania, Diane also taught geography courses for the University of Pittsburgh.

A life-long member of United Methodist Women, she has held district offices in UMW, has led numerous mission studies at Regional and Conference Schools of Christian Mission, and is currently the Assistant Dean for the WPA School of Christian Mission and Mission Ambassador for the WPA Annual Conference.

Diane has visited 30 countries (seven continents), connecting with Christians during many of those travel experiences. She has participated in four international courses on Lay Leadership Training sponsored by the World Council of Churches.

ADDITIONAL RESOURCES

India & Pakistan Map. By Sarla E. Chand. This beautiful four-color map, 22³/₄" x 33", shows topography, provinces, and major cities in India and Pakistan in relation to other Asian countries. Eight panels on the reverse side provide a ready reference to history, current statistics, religion, mission projects, and basic geographic facts for both India and Pakistan. The map may be used in conjunction with the adult study book and video or as a valuable resource on its own. **(Eng. #3692) $8.95**

Video for 2005 Mission Studies. This fast-paced video gives further perspective on the three mission study themes for 2005: Children of the Bible, India & Pakistan, and Public Education. The video can be used in conjunction with the mission study book or as a discussion starter on any of the three topics. A study guide is included. Approximately 40 minutes. **(#3656) $19.95**

India & Pakistan. By Glory Dharmaraj. This four-page reprint of the 2005-2006 mission study in Spanish and Korean gives an insightful summary of the history, people, and religion of the region.
(Span. #5726) Free for postage and handling
(Kor. #5727) Free for postage and handling

Response, May 2005. This special issue of the magazine will be a resource for the India & Pakistan mission study. **(#3671) $1.75**

New World Outlook, May/June 2005. This special issue of the magazine will be a supplement to the mission study with reports from United Methodist churches in India and Pakistan. **(#3683) $3.00**

Please mail order with check payable to:
SERVICE CENTER
GENERAL BOARD OF GLOBAL MINISTRIES
7820 READING RD CALLER NO 1800
CINCINNATI OH 45222-1800

Costs for shipping and handling:

Sale Items:	Free Items:
$25 or less, add $4.65	50 or less, add $3.50
$25.01-$60, add $5.75	51-400, add $4.50
$60.01-$100, add $7.00	Over 400, add $1.50 per 100
Over $100, add 6.5%	

If billing is preferred, a $2.00 billing fee is charged in addition to shipping and handling.

For billed or credit card orders:
WEB ADDRESS: www.scorders.org
E-MAIL: scorders@gbgm-umc.org
CALL TOLL-FREE: 1-800-305-9857
FAX ORDERS: 1-513-761-3722

Price $7.50

Stock #3649